"The Sociology of Information Technology"

GoodMan, Volume 1

Patrick Mukosha

Published by Patrick Mukosha, 2024.

Title: "The Sociology of Information Technology":

Copyright Notice

All Rights Reserved.

No part of this publication may be reproduced, or stored in a database or retrieval system, or transmitted, in any form or by any means, electronic, mechanical, photocopying, recording, or otherwise, without the prior written permission of the publisher. No patent liability is assumed with respect to the use of the information contained herein.

Although every precaution has been taken in the preparation of this book, the author and publisher assume no responsibility for the errors or omissions. Neither is any liability assumed resulting from the use of the information contained herein.

Copyright 2024© Dr. Patrick Mukosha
First published: June, 2024
Publisher: Patrick Mukosha PhD

Trademarks

All terms mentioned in this book that are known to be trademarks or service marks have been appropriately capitalized. The Author and the publisher cannot attest to the accuracy of this information. Use of a term in this book should not be regarded as affecting the validity of any trademark or service mark.

Warning and Disclaimer

Every effort has been made to make this book as complete and as accurate as possible, but no warranty or fitness is implied. The information provided in this book is on as is basis. The Author and the Publisher shall have neither liability nor responsibility to any person or entity with respect to any loss or damage arising from the use the information contained in this book.

Author: Patrick Chisenga Mukosha PhD

Acknowledgements

The author is indebted to a large number of researchers, and consultants in the field of Information Technology (Sociology and Information Technology) whose works were referred to in writing this book – and appears below and in the bibliography.

The author also would like to acknowledge the encouragement of my wife; Gracious Lumba Maboshe-Mukosha, and my children, whose comments and constructive criticism kept the author alive. The author also benefitted from the comments of several of my Sociology and ICT colleagues. They generously shared their insights and experiences in an evolving field where tacit knowledge is indispensable.

Special thanks go to Lionel Hugh Weston; an Educationalist, British National, my former Secondary School Teacher and Guardian, without whom I would never have had a strong education foundation in life. His contribution in my education career is immeasurable. I shall forever remain indebted to him and the entire Weston's family.

Abstract

"The Sociology of Information Technology" explores the complex interplay between technology and society, showing how social structures, conventions, and interactions are shaped by and shaped by information technology breakthroughs. By means of an extensive analysis of past viewpoints, conceptual models, and current concerns, this book provides an understanding of the complex effects of technology on several facets of human existence.

The book starts out by *outlining the basic ideas of information technology sociology*, highlighting how society and technology are mutually dependent. The historical development of information technology is then traced, stressing significant changes in society along the way, from the printing press' invention to the internet's launch and beyond.

With a *focus on several theoretical frameworks* such as conflict theory, functionalism, and symbolic interactionism, the *book offers analytical instruments to comprehend the intricate relationships between technology and society*. It looks at how differences in access to technology and its effects on social stratification are examined, as well as how socioeconomic factors contribute to the digital divide.

A thorough examination is conducted of the *effects of information technology on politics, health, education, social interaction, work, and culture*. The book covers the entire gamut of the digital age, from the emergence of social networks and online communities to the moral conundrums related to privacy and monitoring.

The urgent concerns covered include *cybersecurity, globalization, environmental effects, cybercrime, and ethical issues*. These should cause readers to critically explore the societal implications of technology and the moral obligations of those who build, use, and regulate it.

The book's last chapters make predictions about *probable developments in the sociology of information technology*, stressing the opportunities, problems, and possible social effects of emerging technologies.

"The Sociology of Information Technology" is a must-read for academics, professionals, and students who want to comprehend and navigate the digital age since it provides a thorough account of the intricate interactions that exist between technology and society. This book challenges readers to think critically about the societal ramifications of information technology and to imagine paths towards a more equitable future through its interdisciplinary approach and nuanced analysis.

Chapter 1: Introduction to the Sociology of Information Technology

1.1. Understanding the Intersection of Society and Technology

Technology and society have a closely entwined relationship that has changed dramatically over time. At first, *technology was used to provide food, provide shelter, and facilitate communication*—basic human needs. But as civilizations developed, *technology advanced in complexity and started influencing social structures, cultural norms, and behavioural patterns.*

The way societies operate has been profoundly altered by important historical turning points like the Industrial Revolution, the printing press, and the internet. Every technology development altered how humans interacted, worked, communicated, and even perceived the world. For example, *the internet transformed international trade and communication, creating a society that is increasingly linked and information-rich.*

These days, technology influences every part of our lives, from how we work and amuse ourselves to how we stay in touch with people and obtain information. *Blockchain, the Internet of Things, and artificial intelligence are examples of emerging technologies that have the potential to further transform civilization.*

Understanding Science, Technology, and Society (STS) is the focus of this book. STS is an interdisciplinary field of study that looks at how scientific advancements and technological developments affect society and vice versa. Modernization theory, social constructivism, and path dependence are a few of the theories related to STS. Using a theoretical lens to examine the advancement of science and technology helps scholars better comprehend trends and indicators of future progress. In relation to STS, ideas like race and gender are also examined in order to give a full circle understanding of the STS concept.

1.2. What Role Does Science and Technology Play in Modern Society?

The growth and development of contemporary society are largely dependent on science and technology. They solve important difficulties, stimulate innovation, and enhance quality of life. The ways that science and technology influence several facets of societal evolution are examined in detail below, with pertinent examples to highlight their significance.

1.2.1. Economic Growth and Development:

1. **Industry and Innovation:**

- **Example:** An illustration would be the growth of Silicon Valley's tech sector.
- **Justification:** Innovation is sparked by science and technology and results in the development of new markets and employment opportunities. Known for its start-ups and technological innovations, Silicon Valley has developed into a global centre for economic growth, drawing capital and talent from all over the world.

1. **Efficiency and Productivity:**

- **Example:** Manufacturing automation is one example.
- **Explanation:** By automating repetitive processes, decreasing errors, and cutting manufacturing costs, technologies like robotics and AI improve productivity. Competitiveness and economic output are increased by this efficiency.

1.2.2. Medical Care and Medicines

1. **Medical Advancements:**

- **Example:** Vaccine development, such as the COVID-19 vaccine.
- **Justification:** The invention of vaccinations, which have prevented the spread of infectious illnesses and saved millions of lives, is the result of scientific study and technological developments. The quick development of COVID-19 vaccinations is an example of how technology and science may respond to international health emergencies.

1. **Medical Technologies:**

- **Example:** For instance, CT and MRI scanners.
- **Justification:** State-of-the-art medical technology facilitate precise disease detection and efficient treatment. Non-invasive internal examinations made possible by MRI and CT scanners promote early detection and improved patient outcomes.

1.2.3. Connectivity and Communication

1. **Global Communication:**

- **Example:** Mobile networks and the internet are two examples.
- **Justification:** The internet has completely changed communication by enabling instantaneous connections with people all over the world. Mobile networks have improved connectivity even more, making it possible to communicate and access information even on the road.

1. **Social Media and Information Exchange:**

- **Example:** Examples of these platforms include YouTube, Facebook, and Twitter.
- **Justification:** Social media sites allow for the quick exchange of ideas and information, which promotes international dialogue and cooperation. They are now effective instruments for awareness-raising and social change.

1.2.4. Education and Information Sharing

1. **Online Education and E-Learning:**

- **Example:** Massive Open Online Courses (MOOCs) such as edX and Coursera are one example.
- **Justification:** By removing financial and geographic constraints, online education platforms enable people all around the world to have access to high-quality education. MOOCs provide courses from prestigious universities, promoting skill development and lifetime learning.

1. **Educational Technologies:**

- **Example:** Khan Academy is one example of an interactive learning platform.
- **Justification:** Interactive and customized learning is made possible by digital tools and platforms. For example, Khan Academy provides interactive exercises and instructional films on a variety of disciplines.

1.2.5. Environmental Protection and Sustainable Development

1. **Renewable Technologies:**

- **Example:** Wind turbines and solar panels are two examples.
- **Justification:** The development of renewable energy technology is essential to the goal of sustainable development. Clean energy sources like solar and wind turbines lessen reliance on fossil fuels and help to slow down global warming.

1. **Environmental Surveillance:**

- **Example:** Examples include remote sensing devices and satellite photography.
- **Justification:** These technologies make it possible to track changes in the environment, including pollution, deforestation, and climatic patterns. The creation of successful environmental policies and conservation plans is aided by accurate data.

1.2.6. Infrastructure and Transportation:

1. **Advanced Transportation Systems:**

- **Example:** Autonomous and electric cars are two examples.
- **Justification:** Transportation technology advancements like electric and self-driving vehicles increase productivity, cut pollutants, and boost security. Leading companies in the development of these advanced technologies are Tesla and others.

1. **Smart Cities:**

- **Example:** An illustration would be integrated public services and traffic management systems.
- **Explanation:** Traffic management, energy distribution, and public safety are just a few of the services that smart city

technologies integrate and optimize using the Internet of Things. Better resource management and living conditions in cities result from this.

1.2.7. Improving Quality of Life:

1. **Consumer Technology:**

- **Example:** Examples are smart home appliances and smartphones.
- **Justification:** Convenience, connectivity, and entertainment are three ways that consumer electronics enhance everyday living. Smartphones are now necessary for business, play, and communication, while smart home appliances improve living spaces with automation and remote control.

1. **Media and Entertainment:**

- **Example:** Gaming platforms and streaming services such as Netflix are two examples.
- **Justification:** Diverse and immersive experiences are made possible by technological improvements in entertainment. While gaming platforms offer social interaction and interactive enjoyment, streaming services give content that is available whenever it's needed.

In summary, modern civilization is built on the foundations of science and technology, which propel advancement in many fields. They make it possible for the economy to expand, improve healthcare, foster better communication, progress education, encourage sustainability, transform transportation, and raise people's standard of living. The future is still being shaped by the advancement and integration of science and technology, which is tackling global issues and opening up new avenues for development and innovation. We create the conditions for a prosperous and sustainable future by encouraging a culture that values scientific research and technical advancement.

14

1.3. IT Professionals Must Comprehend This Intersection:

The social issues that come up in daily life serve as an inspiration for creativity. Technology helps us get beyond barriers that restrict our capabilities. Social determinism holds that technological advancements are made in response to the demands and preferences of society.

Therefore, understanding how society and technology interact is essential for IT professionals for a number of reasons:

1.3.1. **Creating Relevant Solutions:** IT professionals can create technological solutions that are more significant and relevant by having a thorough awareness of society's demands, beliefs, and behaviours. *Taking into account the societal context when creating software programs, creating user interfaces, or putting cybersecurity measures in place guarantees that technology effectively meets the needs of users.*

1.3.2. **Reducing Adverse Effects**: Technology may have unanticipated effects on society that include escalating inequality, violating private rights, or sustaining prejudices. IT professionals are essential in recognizing and reducing these detrimental effects through responsible innovation, ethical design, and policy advocacy for diversity and fairness.

1.3.3. **Facilitating Digital Transformation:** To remain competitive and relevant in the modern digital era, firms in every industry are undertaking digital transformation. As major forces behind this change, *IT professionals must comprehend cultural trends and preferences in order to create* *strategies that meet changing expectations from society and consumers.*

1.3.4. Handling Ethical Dilemmas: As technology is developed and implemented, ethical issues become more crucial. IT professionals frequently encounter moral conundrums involving data protection and algorithmic prejudice that call for a thorough comprehension of cultural norms and values. IT professionals can sustain ethical standards in their job and make more informed decisions by tackling these issues.

Essentially, *knowing how society and technology interact enables IT professionals to develop more responsible and significant technological solutions that have a good influence on people, businesses, and society at large.*

1.4. Sociology of Information Technology – What is it?

A basic grasp of the ways in which technology interacts with social structures, norms, and behaviors can be obtained by introducing the sociology of information technology.

This is a synopsis:

1.4.1. Definition and Extent: The *Sociology of Information Technology* studies how human civilizations and technical advancements interact. It includes both the historical evolution of technology and current concerns about the interconnectedness of the world. Scholars working in this area investigate how digital technologies affect social dynamics, resource accessibility, and pre-existing scale hierarchies. Thus, *Sociology of Information Technology* examines the social aspects of technology, with a particular emphasis on the interactions between IT networks, devices, and systems and society. It *looks at how social processes—such as political, economic, cultural, and organizational dynamics—shape technology and are shaped by it.*

1.4.1.1. Key Concepts:

- **Technological Determinism:** This theory postulates that technology influences human behaviour and propels social change. It *discusses whether society drives the advancement and application of technology or if technology dictates social results.*
- **Social Construction Technology (SCOT):** SCOT highlights how social variables impact technology's creation, application, and design. It emphasizes how technology are social constructs that mirror societal values, interests, and

power structures rather than being neutral.

- **Digital Divide:** Inequalities in access to and usage of information and communication technologies (ICTs) are referred to as the "*digital divide.*" It includes differences in digital literacy, internet access, and the capacity to use technology for both social and commercial gain.

- **Network Society:** The term "*Network Society,*" which was first used by sociologist Manuel Castells, *refers to a social structure in which networked communication technologies have a ubiquitous influence.* The significance of networks in forming identities, power hierarchies, and social interactions is emphasized.

- **Surveillance Society:** Massively parallel data collecting, monitoring, and analysis is made possible by pervasive digital technologies in this society. Concerns concerning autonomy, privacy, and the effects of surveillance on social control and democracy are brought up by this.

1.4.1.2. Societal Implications:

- **Social Inequality:** The use of information technology has the potential to both worsen and improve current social inequities. It affects socioeconomic results by affecting access to healthcare, work prospects, education, and political engagement.

- **Cultural Transformation:** Technology has a transformative effect on cultural practices, conventions, and identities. It influences entertainment, communication, and the emergence of online communities, promoting the globalization and hybridization of cultures.

- **Political Power Dynamics:** Politics, activism, and governance frameworks are all impacted by information technology. It affects democracy and the allocation of power by making new types of political engagement, monitoring, censorship, and control possible.

1.4.1.3. Challenges and Opportunities:

- **Ethical Dilemmas:** As technology develops and is used more widely, ethical questions about digital rights, privacy, surveillance, data ownership, and algorithmic prejudice are brought up.
- **Digital Rights and Governance:** International collaboration, legal frameworks, and public involvement are necessary to guarantee digital rights, cybersecurity, and accountability in the digital era.
- **Responsible Innovation:** Encouraging responsible innovation means taking into account how technology will affect society at every stage of the process—from design to development to implementation. Stakeholder participation, interdisciplinary cooperation, and a dedication to moral standards are necessary.

Navigating the intricate interactions between technology and society requires an understanding of information technology sociology. It fosters a more just, inclusive, and sustainable digital future by empowering people, organizations, and policymakers to foresee and address the societal ramifications of technical breakthroughs.

1.5. The Role of Technology in Shaping Society

The new information and communication technologies' (ICTs') technological characteristics are beginning to take center stage in explanations of modern development and change. Many sociologists believe that the most important social trends and changes have their roots in technology.

I would also add to this a *propensity to interpret or conceive these technologies in terms of their technical characteristics and to establish their relationship to the sociological domain in terms of their uses and effects.* The task facing sociology is not so much to downplay the importance of technology as it is to provide analytical frameworks that enable us to comprehend the intricate interactions between technology and society.

Technology has a significant impact on how society is shaped in many ways, including how individuals connect, communicate, work, and live their lives. Technology, from antiquated instruments to contemporary digital advancements, has played a pivotal role in propelling societal advancement and metamorphosis.

Here is a synopsis:

1.5.1. **Economic Impact:** Technology stimulates economic growth by raising industry-wide productivity, efficiency, and innovation. Artificial intelligence (AI), robotics, and automation are changing the nature of employment, which is *displacing workers in some industries and opening up new ones in others.* Online marketplaces, digital payment methods, and e-commerce platforms have transformed international trade and commerce while increasing consumer choice and market reach.

1.5.2. **Social Impact:** Through messaging apps, social media, and online communities, *technology helps people communicate and interact with one another.* Social networking sites have revolutionized the way individuals communicate, exchange knowledge, and organize for social issues, influencing group identities and movements. Digital technologies have also had an impact on relationships, societal conventions, and behaviours. These effects range from altered family dynamics to altered dating patterns.

1.5.3. **Cultural Impact:** Through internet content, entertainment platforms, and digital media, *technology affects how culture is expressed, consumed, and disseminated.* Social networking platforms, digital publishing, and streaming services have made it easier for people of all backgrounds to access culture and have their voices heard. But even in the digital age, worries about cultural uniformity, digital piracy, and the decline of traditional cultural traditions remain.

1.5.4. **Political Impact:** Through social media campaigns, online forums, and digital advocacy platforms, *technology enables citizens to participate in politics, activism, and civic life.* Governments may improve public services, increase transparency, and support e-governance projects with the use of digital tools. However, technology also brings up issues of censorship, monitoring, and political information manipulation, underscoring the necessity of digital literacy and moral governing structures.

1.5.5. **Environmental Impact:** *Environmental problems including pollution, resource depletion, and climate change are both exacerbated and lessened by technology.* There are potential to solve environmental issues and foster ecological resilience through the use of green technologies, renewable energy sources, and sustainable activities. However, the increase in energy use, digital carbon footprints, and technological trash present serious environmental problems that need for creative solutions and conscientious consumer habits.

To sum up, Technology has a wide range of effects on society, influencing social, political, cultural, economic, and environmental dynamics. In order to fully utilize technology's revolutionary potential while reducing its negative effects and promoting a more inclusive, fair, and sustainable future for all, it is imperative to comprehend the intricate interactions that exist between technology and society.

1.6. Social Impacts of Information Technology

Here is a succinct summary of how Information Technology (IT) is becoming more and more integrated into several facets of society. Understanding how IT affects society is crucial in the current digital era.

1.6.1. Interaction with Others and Communication:

- Contact via social media, video conferencing, email, and instant messaging is facilitated.
- Social interactions are being transformed, making it possible to establish virtual ties and connections across geographic borders.
- Influence on the development of online communities, privacy restrictions, and interpersonal communication abilities.

1.6.2. Online Communities and Social Networking:

- Emergence of social media sites and its impact on social dynamics, such as Facebook, Instagram, and Twitter.
- Formation of virtual communities around common identities, interests, or connections.
- Effects on interpersonal relationships, including as the creation of new bonds, the upkeep of current ones, and the possibility of addiction or social isolation.

1.6.3. The Digital Divide and Information Access

- Expansion of knowledge and information availability via digital and internet resources.

- Persistent differences in digital literacy and access to technology, which fuel the digital divide.
- Consequences that exacerbate social inequality in the areas of civic involvement, work, healthcare, and education.

1.6.4. Employment and Work

- Transformation of the workplace through digital collaboration tools, telecommuting, and remote employment.
- Influence on employment patterns, job marketplaces, and the type of work (such as freelancing and the gig economy).
- Issues with skills mismatch, job displacement, and the necessity of lifelong learning in a quickly changing technological environment.

1.6.5. Privacy and Surveillance

- Worries around digital surveillance technology, surveillance, and data privacy.
- Consequences of governments, businesses, and other groups gathering, tracking, and profiling data.
- Discussions on how to strike a balance between public safety, national security, and individual privacy rights.

1.6.6. Digital Identity and Representation

- Creation and portrayal of identities in digital environments, such as digital personas, avatars, and social media profiles.
- Challenges pertaining to cyberbullying, harassment, and identity theft online.
- Investigation of the potential effects of *Augmented Reality* (AR) and *Virtual Reality* (VR) technology on social interactions and self-perception.

1.6.7. Activism and Social Justice

- Technology use in advocacy campaigns, activism, and social justice initiatives.
- Examples of social media mobilization for social change, online petitions, and digital activism.
- Digital activism's drawbacks and obstacles, such as echo chambers, algorithmic bias, and online censorship.

In summary, an overview of the ways that information technology has affected society in the areas of activism, employment, privacy, social networking, communication, and the digital divide. A call to action to solve social injustices, advance digital literacy, and maximize technology's beneficial effects for a society that is more fair and inclusive.

1.7. Technological Impacts on Cultural Norms and Values

This is a conversation about *how technology affects cultural norms and values*. Members of a society shape each other's identities, interactions, and perceptions through common cultural norms and values, which are fundamental beliefs and behaviours. Because it has changed the way individuals interact with cultural traditions, communicate, and consume information, *technology has a big impact on cultural norms and values.*

1.7.1. Social Interaction and Communication:

- Through social media, messaging apps, and email, communication may now happen instantly and globally thanks to technology.
- Language use has changed as a result of the growth of digital communication platforms, giving rise to new slang phrases and communication idioms.
- More people are interacting with and sharing cultural subtleties and expressions, which promotes cross-cultural interactions and language hybridization.

1.7.2. Cultural Representation and Media Consumption:

- People may now access a wider variety of cultural content thanks to digital media platforms, which have made it easier for people to consume media from around the globe.
- Media depictions influence and reinforce cultural norms and values, shaping public perceptions of gender, race, ethnicity, and other social identities.
- The growth of user-generated content and online

communities has made it possible for underrepresented voices and other cultural viewpoints to become more visible.

1.7.3. **Cultural Production and Consumption:**

- Technology has completely changed how culture is produced, distributed, and consumed, upending the established hierarchy of gatekeepers and middlemen.
- The distinction between creators and consumers is blurred by digital tools and platforms that enable anyone to make and distribute cultural products.
- Digital technologies have allowed the cultural industries—music, film, literature, and art—to adapt and create new mediums for artistic expression.

1.7.4. **Heritage and Cultural Preservation:**

- Through digital archives, online repositories, and museums, technology contributes to the preservation and dissemination of cultural heritage.
- Technologies such as *Augmented Reality* (AR) and *Virtual Reality* (VR) provide immersive experiences that support historic tourism and improve cultural preservation initiatives.
- Digital platforms promote cross-cultural understanding and appreciation by facilitating cultural exchange and collaboration among communities.

1.7.5. **Challenges and Controversies:**

- Concerns over cultural homogenization are sparked by technological improvements since local customs and languages are subordinated to international media content and prevailing cultural narratives.

- The phenomenon of *cultural appropriation* and *misrepresentation* in digital environments underscores the imperative nature of ethical deliberations and sensitivity to a range of cultural viewpoints.
- For the cultural industries and artists, issues with digital piracy, copyright violations, and intellectual property rights present difficulties.

1.7.6. Resistance and Adaptation to Culture:

- As societies negotiate the conflicts between embracing new technologies and maintaining traditional customs, resistance and adaptation processes result.
- Adoption rates and usage patterns are influenced by cultural norms and values, which also determine people's attitudes and behaviours around the adoption of technology.
- Movements for cultural resistance, such those advocating for a digital detox or regaining cultural sovereignty online, are a reflection of larger discussions over how technology affects cultural identity.

To sum up, Technology has a significant impact on cultural norms and values because it changes how people communicate, consume media, produce culture, preserve it, and adapt it. Promoting cultural diversity, inclusivity, and moral use of technology while navigating the challenges of cultural change in the digital era requires an understanding of these relationships.

1.8. Ethical and Moral Considerations in the Use of Technology

In today's linked world, using technology with ethics and morality in mind is crucial. It is imperative for an IT professional to comprehend and tackle these factors in order to guarantee that technology is utilized for the betterment of society.

Here is a thorough explanation of a few important points:

1.8.1. Privacy and Data Protection: The gathering, storing, and usage of personal data raises a number of serious ethical issues in technology. Respecting people's right to privacy and making ensuring that data is handled securely and openly are essential. This entails putting strong data protection procedures in place, getting informed consent before collecting data, and granting people control over their data.

1.8.2. Security: It is not just a technical problem but also an ethical requirement to ensure the security of digital systems and information. Cybersecurity lapses can have disastrous repercussions, from monetary loss to life-threatening situations. In order to defend against cyber threats, IT workers have a moral duty to give top priority to security measures including encryption, access limits, and recurring security assessments.

1.8.3. Inclusivity and Accessibility: Regardless of a person's ability or financial situation, technology should be available to all. The goal of IT professionals should be to create inclusive technologies that meet the needs of a wide range of users. This entails putting in place tools for visually impaired users, such as screen readers, captioning movies, and creating user interfaces that are simple to use and understand for those with disabilities.

1.8.4. **Algorithmic Bias and Fairness:** Concern over algorithmic bias is developing as AI and machine learning algorithms become more and more integrated into decision-making processes. IT specialists must make sure algorithms are educated on objective facts and do not reinforce or worsen already-existing social injustices. This entails putting fairness mechanisms in place, auditing algorithms on a regular basis, and offering transparency into the decision-making process.

1.8.5. **Environmental Impact:** With technology developing so quickly, there are worries about how it may affect the environment, especially in terms of energy use and electronic waste. IT workers should try to reduce their carbon footprint and take the environmental sustainability of their initiatives into account. This can involve encouraging recycling and ethical behaviour, employing renewable energy sources for data centres, and optimizing software for energy efficiency.

1.8.6. **Digital Divide:** The difference between people who have access to technology and the internet and those who do not is known as the "digital divide." By encouraging digital literacy, increasing internet access in underprivileged areas, and creating reasonably priced technology solutions that meet the needs of excluded groups, IT professionals should try to close this gap.

1.8.7. **Ethical AI and Automation:** As AI and automation become more prevalent, ethical questions about employment displacement, accountability, and the moral application of AI in decision-making processes arise. In order to ensure that AI systems are used responsibly and transparently, IT professionals should be aware of the social and ethical implications of these technologies. This could entail creating moral standards for AI research, adding human oversight to automated processes, and resolving employment-related issues.

1.8.8. **Global Impact:** The influence of technology is not limited by national boundaries, as it can have far-reaching effects on a worldwide level. IT workers should think about how their job will affect the world at large, including concerns about internet governance, digital rights, and geopolitical tensions. This could entail supporting laws that support an unrestricted and open internet, taking cultural variations into account when designing technology, and working with foreign partners to address global issues.

To sum up, moral and ethical issues are essential to using technology responsibly. When it comes to making sure that technology advances society and preserves core moral values like sustainability, fairness, privacy, and inclusivity, IT professionals are indispensable. IT professionals can contribute to the creation of a more moral and just society by making these factors a priority in their work.

1.9. Technological Innovation and Social Progress

I vouch for the significant influence that technical innovation has on the advancement of society. Technology and society have a complicated and nuanced relationship, with new developments in technology frequently acting as catalysts for constructive societal change. The following is a thorough explanation of how technology innovation propels social progress:

1.9.1. **Improved Access to Information:** The internet in particular has completely changed how people can obtain information. By giving people unparalleled access to news, cultural content, and educational resources, it has democratized knowledge. More literacy, knowledge, and empowerment within society are fostered by this improved access to information, which eventually propels social progress.

1.9.2. **Enhanced Connectivity and Communication:** Social media, messaging applications, and video conferencing platforms are just a few examples of the technologies that have revolutionized how people interact and communicate with one another. They make it possible for people to stay in contact with friends and relatives who live on the other side of the world, they help professionals collaborate and share knowledge, and they provide marginalized communities the voice and strength to demand change.

1.9.3. **Economic Empowerment:** Innovation in technology has the power to launch new businesses, produce jobs, and boost the economy. It encourages innovation and entrepreneurship, empowering people to launch and grow new companies. Furthermore, digital marketplaces and platforms give small companies and micro-entrepreneurs the chance to connect with a worldwide audience, lowering entry barriers and advancing economic inclusion.

1.9.4. Advances in Healthcare: The use of technology has completely changed the way that healthcare is delivered, improving patient outcomes, expanding access to care, and increasing system efficiency. The delivery and management of healthcare have been revolutionized by innovations like telemedicine, wearable technology, electronic health records, and medical imaging technologies, which have improved public health and quality of life in the process.

1.9.5. Education Transformation: By enhancing accessibility, engagement, and personalization, technology has the capacity to completely transform education. The ability to access educational content at any time and from any location is provided to learners through digital learning platforms, online courses, and educational apps. Furthermore, immersive learning experiences can be produced with the use of technologies like virtual reality (VR) and augmented reality (AR), which improve understanding and retention.

1.9.6. Environmental Sustainability: Addressing environmental issues and advancing sustainability are made possible by technological innovation. The move to a more sustainable energy system is made possible by developments in smart infrastructure, energy-efficient manufacturing techniques, and renewable energy technology. Furthermore, technology like big data analytics, remote sensing, and IoT (Internet of Things) devices make it easier to monitor and manage natural resources, which promotes sustainable resource usage and better decision-making.

1.9.7. **Social Justice and Equity:** By encouraging openness, responsibility, and inclusivity, technology can be a potent instrument for furthering these goals. Social media platforms have played a crucial role in bringing social concerns to the public's attention, organizing grassroots movements, and holding institutions responsible for their deeds. Furthermore, innovations like blockchain have chances to address trust and transparency concerns in a number of industries, such as supply chains, banking, and governance.

1.9.8. **Cultural interchange and Understanding:** Technology removes linguistic and geographic obstacles to promote cultural interchange and understanding. Individuals from different origins can interact, exchange experiences, and celebrate cultural variety through social media platforms, online forums, and digital content sharing. This ultimately contributes to a more inclusive and harmonious society by fostering empathy, tolerance, and mutual understanding.

To sum up, technological innovation is essential to the advancement of social justice, economic growth, healthcare, education, and the environment. It also fosters individual empowerment and facilitates cross-cultural exchange. But it's important to understand that not everyone benefits equally from technology, and that there are risks and difficulties that come along with it, such the digital divide, privacy issues, and moral ramifications. As information technology specialists, it is our duty to maximize technology's positive effects while reducing any potential drawbacks in order to guarantee that technical advancements will continue to spur constructive social development.

35

1.10. The Importance of Studying Information Technology from a Sociological Perspective

Understanding the complex interaction between technology and society requires an understanding of information technology from a social perspective. A sociological approach explores more deeply into the social, cultural, and ethical aspects of technology, whereas standard IT education frequently concentrates on technical skills and problem-solving abilities. The following justifies the significance of researching information technology from a sociological angle:

1.10.1. **Comprehending Technology Adoption and Use:** Sociological viewpoints contribute to the understanding of why specific technologies are embraced or rejected by society. How people and groups use technology is influenced by a variety of factors, including social networks, political dynamics, economic limitations, and cultural standards. IT specialists may better understand the human aspect of technology adoption by researching these variables, which is crucial for creating technological solutions that are both user-friendly and culturally relevant.

1.10.2. **Analysing Power Dynamics and Inequality:** Social and political influences shape technology; it is not neutral. The creation, development, and application of technology are influenced by power dynamics, socioeconomic inequality, and structural discrepancies, as revealed by sociological analysis. IT workers can contribute to the development of more equitable and inclusive technical solutions that meet the needs of marginalized communities and subvert established power structures by critically analysing these problems.

1.10.3. Examining Access and Digital Divide Issues: The difference in access to technology and the internet between those who don't and those who do is known as the "digital divide." The underlying factors that contribute to digital inequality, such as socioeconomic status, geography, race, gender, age, and education, are clarified by sociological viewpoints. IT specialists can create plans to close the digital gap and encourage digital inclusion for all societal members by researching these variables.

1.10.4. Handling Ethical and Moral Dilemmas: Beyond purely technical concerns, technology presents intricate ethical and moral conundrums. IT workers can better navigate these issues by considering the wider societal effects of technology use via the lens of sociological perspectives. This covers matters like algorithmic bias, data ownership, privacy, spying, and the effect of automation on jobs. IT professionals may create ethical technology solutions that respect human rights and uphold ethical ideals by critically analysing these ethical concerns.

1.10.5. Encouraging Cultural Sensitivity and variety: Sociological viewpoints place a strong emphasis on the value of variety and cultural sensitivity in the development and application of technology. People's perceptions of and interactions with technology are shaped by cultural influences; if these differences are not taken into consideration, design biases and unexpected consequences may result. IT workers may create inclusive, culturally sensitive technologies that appeal to a wide range of user groups and uphold cultural norms and values by researching sociocultural factors.

1.10.6. **Improving Stakeholder Engagement and Collaboration:** Technology initiatives are by their very nature social undertakings involving cooperation between a variety of stakeholders, such as advocacy organizations, legislators, community leaders, and end users. Sociological viewpoints highlight the significance of stakeholder participation and involvement. IT professionals may make sure that the final products and services satisfy the needs and preferences of all stakeholders by incorporating stakeholders from a variety of backgrounds in the design and implementation of technological solutions.

1.10.7. **Promoting Critical Thought and Reflection:** Sociological viewpoints promote critical thinking as well as thoughtful consideration of the ethical and social ramifications of technology. IT workers can have a more comprehensive grasp of how technology affects society and learn to assess technical advancements critically by interacting with sociological theories, case studies, and practical examples. IT workers may predict possible outcomes, reduce risks, and make well-informed decisions that support larger society objectives and values by using this critical lens.

In conclusion, comprehending the intricate interactions between technology and society requires a sociological understanding of information technology. IT professionals can create more comprehensive, responsible, and socially conscious approaches to technology design, development, and implementation by looking at topics like technology adoption, power dynamics, digital inequality, ethical conundrums, cultural sensitivity, stakeholder engagement, and critical reflection. This multidisciplinary approach not only improves technical proficiency but also gives IT workers the know-how to tackle the more significant ethical and social issues of the digital age.

39

1.11. Towards a Holistic Understanding of the Intersection of Society and Technology

It is critical for IT specialists and professionals to work toward a comprehensive knowledge of the nexus between society and technology. This all-encompassing comprehension spans multiple facets, encompassing *social, cultural, political, economic, and ethical elements.* IT workers may aid in the creation of *technology that is not just technically sound but also morally and socially conscious by recognizing and resolving these interconnections.*

Below is a thorough summary of the main ideas covered:

1.11.1. Sociotechnical Perspective: Adopting a sociotechnical perspective recognizes the close *connections between technology and cultural norms, social institutions, and human behaviour.* grasp how technical breakthroughs shape society and vice versa requires a grasp of the reciprocal interaction between society and technology.

1.11.2. Technology's Social Repercussions: Beyond its technical applications, *technology* has significant social ramifications. It *affects how people engage with one another, communicate, work, and learn.* IT experts may foresee possible outcomes, recognize moral conundrums, and provide technological solutions that are consistent with larger society objectives and ideals by researching these social ramifications.

1.11.3. Ethical Issues: The proper development and application of technology heavily relies on ethical issues. The ethical ramifications of their job, including *concerns about* *algorithmic bias, privacy, data security, and digital rights, must be taken into account by IT workers.* Within the digital ecosystem, IT professionals may foster trust, accountability, and transparency by adhering to ethical principles and values.

1.11.4. Cultural Sensitivity and Inclusivity: In order to create technology that appeals to a wide range of user demographics, cultural sensitivity and inclusivity are crucial. When creating technological solutions, *IT professionals should take user preferences, social settings, and cultural differences into account.* IT workers may develop technology that represents the needs, values, and viewpoints of all stakeholders by embracing diversity and inclusivity.

1.11.5. Digital Divide and Access Issues: IT workers need to focus on bridging the digital divide and advancing digital inclusion as important concerns. For technology to benefit everyone in society, *access constraints like lack of digital literacy, geographic restrictions, and socioeconomic gaps must be addressed.* Expanding digital equity and underprivileged groups' access to technology can be greatly aided by IT professionals.

1.11.6. Collaboration and Stakeholder involvement: Developing technology solutions that satisfy the requirements of many user groups requires collaboration and stakeholder involvement. IT experts should *include end users, legislators, community leaders, and advocacy groups, among other stakeholders, in the design and implementation process.* IT professionals may guarantee that technological solutions are sustainable, inclusive, and relevant by promoting cooperation and participatory design methodologies.

1.11.7. Continuous Learning and Adaptation: The relationship between technology and society is dynamic and ever-changing. To keep up with new trends, cultural changes, and technical breakthroughs, *IT workers need to be lifelong learners and adapters*. IT workers may stay adaptable and sensitive to the shifting demands and obstacles of the digital era by fostering a culture of innovation and lifelong learning.

In conclusion, IT professionals who want to use their work to positively influence society must adopt a comprehensive grasp of the nexus between society and technology. Through the consideration of sociocultural dynamics, ethical implications, inclusion, cooperation, and continuous learning, information technology professionals can create technological solutions that foster community building, individual empowerment, and the advancement of a more sustainable and equitable future for all.

Chapter 2: Historical Perspectives on Information Technology

43

2.1. Historical Perspectives: Tracing the Evolution of Information Technology

Understanding how information technology (IT) has changed over time in response to societal demands, historical developments, and technological advancements is made possible by tracking the field's progress. For IT professionals to appreciate the context in which modern technology operates and to predict future trends, it is imperative that they comprehend this progression.

Let's examine in-depth the historical viewpoints on the development of IT:

2.1.1. Era Prior to Modern (Pre-20th Century):

- **Ancient Tools and Writing Systems:** Writing systems, abacuses, and early forms of computation are examples of instruments that people used in ancient civilizations to record and transfer information. These tools are the origins of information technology.

- **Printing Press:** Johannes Gutenberg's creation of the printing press in the fifteenth century transformed the way information was disseminated by making it more readily available and reasonably priced. This was a major turning point in the history of information technology, setting the stage for printed products like books and newspapers to be produced in large quantities.

2.1.2. Early Computing Devices (20th-Century):

- **Mechanical Calculators:** The basis for contemporary computing was established in the late 19th and early 20th centuries with the development of mechanical calculators like the Pascaline and the Difference Engine, which automated mathematical calculations.

- **Electromechanical Computers:** The Harvard Mark I and the ENIAC were two examples of the electromechanical computers developed in the middle of the 20th century. These early computers were big, heavy devices that carried out calculations using relays and vacuum tubes.
- **Transistors and Integrated Circuits:** By making computers smaller, quicker, and more dependable, the introduction of the transistor in the late 1940s and the following development of integrated circuits in the 1950s and 1960s revolutionized computing.

2.1.3. Mainframes and Minicomputers (1950s–1970s):

- **Mainframe Computers:** Throughout the 1950s and 60s, mainframe computers dominated the computing world, doing activities including data processing, scientific calculations, and business applications for huge corporations and governmental institutions.
- **Mini Computers:** As more compact and reasonably priced mainframe substitutes, mini computers first appeared in the 1960s and 1970s. They increased access to computing power by being used in smaller firms, universities, and research institutions.

2.1.4. The Internet and Personal Computers (1980s–1990s):

- **Personal Computers (PCs):** Individuals and small businesses were able to access computing power with the arrival of personal computers in the 1980s, particularly the IBM PC and the Apple Macintosh. PCs are now more accessible and user-friendly thanks to the *Graphical User Interface* (GUI) and operating systems like Windows and MS-DOS (*Microsoft Disk Operating System*).

- **World Wide Web and Internet:** The late 20th century saw the emergence of the internet, which completely changed how people communicated and shared information. The World Wide Web (WWW), created by Tim Berners-Lee in 1989, made it possible to create linked hypertext pages, which laid the groundwork for the development of the contemporary internet.

2.1.5. Mobile Computing and The Digital Revolution (21st-Century):

- **Mobile Devices:** The widespread use of *Smartphones* and tablets in the early years of the twenty-first century revolutionized communication and information access. Wireless networks, mobile apps, and mobile computing technologies have made computing ubiquitous and available anywhere, at any time.
- **Cloud Computing:** With the rise of cloud computing in the 2000s, access to computer resources has become more widely available, allowing both individuals and companies to take use of scalable and reasonably priced IT services and infrastructure via the internet.
- **AI and Big Data:** Data analysis and decision-making have been completely transformed by the proliferation of digital data and developments in *Artificial Intelligence* (AI) and *Machine Learning* (ML). *Big Data (BD) technologies stimulate efficiency and creativity in a variety of industries by enabling enterprises to handle, analyse, and extract insights from enormous information.*

2.1.6. Developing Technologies (Former and Present):

- **Internet of Things (IoT):** By linking commonplace items and gadgets, the IoT transforms connectivity by allowing them to gather and share data. Smart homes, healthcare, transportation, agriculture, and industrial automation are just a few industries that can benefit from IoT technologies.
- **Blockchain:** Blockchain technology allows for safe and transparent peer-to-peer transactions without the need for middlemen. It was made popular by cryptocurrencies like Bitcoin. Industries including finance, supply chain management, and healthcare could be affected.
- **Virtual Reality (VR) And Augmented Reality (AR):** These technologies improve human perception and interaction by building *Immersive Virtual Worlds* (VR) or *Superimposing Digital Content On the Real World* (AR). These technologies can be used for entertainment, education, training, gaming, and design.

To sum up, the development of information technology has been marked by constant innovation and change, fueled by developments in networking, hardware, software, and human-computer interaction. IT professionals can better grasp the historical background, technological advancements, and societal influences that have shaped the current digital age by following this evolution.

In the future, developing technologies have the potential to completely transform the way people work, live, and interact. This will provide IT professionals with new opportunities as well as problems that they must overcome in order to advance society.

2.2. Societal Impacts of Key Technological Innovations Throughout History

Technological advancements have shaped people's lives, careers, communication styles, and interactions with the outside world throughout history.

I'll talk about a few significant technological advancements and how they affect society:

2.2.1. Printing Press (15th Century):

- **Societal Impact:** *Johannes Gutenberg's* creation of the printing press in the fifteenth century completely changed how people communicated and shared knowledge. It made knowledge more widely available by facilitating the mass production of books, newspapers, and other printed items.
- **Impact on Society:** The Renaissance, Reformation, and Scientific Revolution were all fuelled in large part by the printing press, which was essential in the dissemination of ideas, literacy, and knowledge. It gave people the freedom to seek information, question authority, and engage in intellectual conversation, which had a significant impact on political, religious, and cultural changes.

2.2.2. Industrial Revolution (18th–19th Century):

- **Societal Impact:** Mechanized production, urbanization, and technological developments were the hallmarks of industrialized economies, which emerged from rural communities throughout the Industrial Revolution.
- **Impact on Society:** As a result of the Industrial Revolution's

disruption of social and economic systems, factories, mass production, and industrial capitalism all rose to prominence. As more individuals moved from rural to urban regions in search of work, it accelerated urbanization. It resulted in social unrest, labour exploitation, and environmental damage in addition to economic expansion and scientific advancement.

2.2.3. Telegraph (19th-Century):

- **Societal Impact:** The telegraph's development allowed for instantaneous long-distance communication via wired electrical signals.
  Impact on Society: By enabling real-time message over great distances, the telegraph reduced the size of the world and sped up the rate of global connectivity, revolutionizing communication. It was essential to trade, diplomacy, and news distribution, and it helped pave the way for later developments in telecommunications.

2.2.4. Telephone (19th-Century):

- **Societal Impact:** Voice transmission over great distances was made possible by *Alexander Graham Bell*'s development of the telephone, which revolutionized communication.
- **Effect on the Community:** Interpersonal communication was transformed by the telephone, which made it possible for individuals to communicate with each other in real time regardless of where they were in the world. It promoted stronger social ties, made corporate transactions easier, and made coordination and decision-making quicker. The telephone evolved into a necessary tool for communication.

2.2.5. Internet and World Wide Web (20th-century):

- **Societal Impact:** By establishing a global network of connected computers, the internet and World Wide Web transformed communication and the availability of information.

- **Impact on Society:** People may now access a wealth of knowledge, connect with people all over the world, and take part in online communities thanks to the internet, which democratized information access. The introduction of hypertext and multimedia material by the World Wide Web revolutionized the ways in which information is shared, accessed, and utilized. It brought about significant social, cultural, and economic transformations by revolutionizing sectors including media, commerce, education, and entertainment.

2.2.6. Mobile Computing with Smartphones (21st-Century):

- **Societal Impact:** People's access to information, communication, and technology use have all changed as a result of the widespread use of smartphones and other mobile computing devices.

- **Impact on Society:** Smartphones are becoming commonplace instruments for productivity, entertainment, communication, and navigation. They have created new services and business models by revolutionizing sectors like healthcare, banking, transportation, and education. Additionally, mobile computing has made it easier to operate remotely and altered social dynamics by obfuscating the boundaries between business and personal life.

2.2.7. Social Media (21st-Century):

- **Societal Impact:** The emergence of social media sites like Facebook, Instagram, and Twitter has changed how individuals interact with content, connect with one another, and share information.
- **Impact on Society:** People may now connect with friends, family, and communities all around the world thanks to social media, which has completely changed communication and social interaction. It is become a potent instrument for public opinion influencing, news distribution, and social movement organization. It has, however, also sparked worries about online abuse, privacy, false information, and the effect of algorithmic content selection on polarization and echo chambers.

2.2.8. Automation and Artificial Intelligence (AI) – (21st Century):

- **Societal Impact:** Developments in automation and artificial intelligence are changing entire sectors of the economy as well as the nature of labour itself.
- **Impact on Society:** Automation and *Artificial Intelligence* (AI) have the potential to boost productivity, efficiency, and innovation in a number of industries, including manufacturing, healthcare, and finance. They also bring up issues with algorithmic bias, economic injustice, employment displacement, and ethical ramifications. To ensure that AI and automation serve the common good, addressing these issues needs thorough consideration of social values, legal frameworks, and ethical principles.

In summary, significant technical advancements throughout history have shaped society and impacted how people live, work, communicate, and engage with one another. Although these developments have greatly benefited society and the economy, they have also created moral, political, and other issues that need for careful thought and responsible leadership.

In order to direct technology's development and application in ways that advance sustainability, justice, and human well-being, IT professionals must have a thorough awareness of the social consequences of technology.

Chapter 3: Theoretical Frameworks in the Sociology of Information Technology

3.1. Functionalism and Information Technology

Functionalism is a sociological paradigm that sees society as an intricate system with interconnected pieces that cooperate to uphold social order and stability. Functionalism, seen through the lens of information technology, sheds light on how IT is used in society to accomplish a variety of purposes and promote stability and social cohesion.

Let's examine functionalism and information technology in greater detail:

3.1.1. Role of Computer Technology in Social Functions:

- *According to functionalism, every element of society—including institutions, customs, and values—serves a distinct purpose that adds to the stability and general well-being of the community.* Information technology performs a variety of roles in society as well, from promoting economic activity and governance to streamlining communication and information transmission.
- For instance, communication tools like messaging apps, social media, and email are essential for tying together communities, businesses, and individuals. This promotes coordination, collaboration, and social engagement. In addition to facilitating online trade, banking, and supply chain management, information technology also promotes economic expansion and prosperity.

3.1.2. Connectivity and Integration:

- *Functionalism places a strong emphasis on how interdependent and interwoven society's many components are.* Comparably, information technology serves as a glue that unites disparate social structures, groups, and people into a unified whole.

- To promote efficiency, collaboration, and coordination within businesses, enterprise systems and cloud computing platforms, for example, facilitate the seamless integration of business processes and information across departments and geographic locations. Social networking sites establish virtual communities that cut over geographic barriers, enabling users to communicate and engage with one another regardless of their actual physical locations.

3.1.3. Social Order and Stability:

- *Functionalism emphasizes how social norms and structures keep society stable and orderly.* Through the provision of tools and systems that facilitate the efficient operation of societal processes and institutions, information technology plays a role in maintaining social stability.
- Information technologies, such as databases, analytics tools, and decision support systems, for instance, assist businesses in making well-informed decisions, allocating resources effectively, and managing operations successfully, all of which improve organizational performance and stability. Government IT systems assist with tasks including public administration, healthcare, and law enforcement while fostering social order and government.

3.1.4. Manifest and Latent Functions:

- *Functionalism makes a distinction between hidden functions, which are inadvertent or unrecognized outcomes, and apparent functions, which are deliberate and acknowledged functions of social institutions or events.*

- Similar to this, information technology frequently has both overt and covert uses in society. For instance, social media platforms clearly serve to promote social contact and communication. They may not always be visible, but they also serve covert purposes including polarizing society, forming public opinion, and establishing societal standards.

3.1.5. Social Change and Adaptation:

- *Functionalism stresses societal stability, but it also acknowledges that societies change throughout time and adjust to new situations.* Information technology, by bringing new tools, systems, and methods of operation, is a major force behind social change and adaptation.
- Artificial intelligence, automation, and the internet of things, for example, are transforming economies, industries, and social norms, resulting in changes to social connections, job patterns, and economic structures. IT professionals are crucial in enabling this adaptability through the creation and application of creative solutions that take advantage of new opportunities and obstacles.

To sum up, functionalism offers a useful paradigm for comprehending how information technology functions in society. IT professionals can obtain insight into the wider societal ramifications of technical advancements and aid in the development of IT systems and solutions that are in line with societal demands and values by examining how IT functions contribute to social integration, stability, and adaptation.

3.2. Conflict Theory Perspectives on Technology

According to conflict theory, social relations and institutions are shaped by power dynamics, and society is marked by conflict and inequality. From the standpoint of information technology, conflict theory sheds light on the ways in which technology can support or subvert established power structures, social inequities, and power dynamics.

Let's take a closer look at the connection between conflict theory and technology:

3.2.1. Power Dynamics in Access and Development of Technology:

- *Power differences between institutions and social groups are emphasized by Conflict Theory.* Power dynamics affect who creates, owns, and manages technological resources as well as who has access to them in the context of technology.
- For instance, wealthy nations and multinational firms frequently control the creation and ownership of cutting-edge technologies, whereas underprivileged populations and developing areas could not have access to digital gadgets and internet connectivity. This unequal distribution of technology resources exacerbates social inequality and maintains digital divides.

3.2.2. Technological Determinism and Social Control:

- The notion that technology independently propels social change is known as *Technological Determinism*, and *Conflict Theory* challenges it. Rather, it contends that technical advancement is influenced by political, social, and economic factors and can be a means of achieving social dominance and control.

- Surveillance systems, face recognition software, and social media algorithms are examples of technologies that powerful players, such as governments and businesses, can employ to monitor, control, and manipulate individuals and populations. This brings up issues with censorship, invasions of privacy, and the degradation of civil freedoms.

3.2.3. Economic and Labour Effects of Automation:

- *Conflict theory examines the effects of technology on labour markets and economic systems, with a focus on automation and artificial intelligence.* It makes the case that technology, particularly for low-skilled workers, might increase economic inequality and cause job displacement.
- The gig economy, labour outsourcing, and the decline of traditional employment prospects in industries like manufacturing, retail, and transportation are all results of automation and digitization. Due to insecure working conditions and pay stagnation faced by marginalized workers, this has contributed to increased social unrest and economic insecurity.

3.2.4. Corporate Dominance and Digital Capitalism:

- Conflict theory studies what is sometimes called "*Digital Capitalism*," or the concentration of money and power in the hands of multinational firms and technology giants. It makes the case that these businesses take advantage of user data, profit from material created by users, and have significant influence on democratic processes and public discourse.

- Due to their extraordinary market domination and data accumulation, platforms like Facebook, Google, and Amazon are able to have a significant impact on media, advertising, and consumer behaviour. Concerns concerning monopolistic behaviour, antitrust laws, and the demise of democratic government are raised by this concentration of power.

3.2.5. Social Movements and Resistance:

- *Conflict theory places a strong emphasis on how social movements and group efforts can be used to oppose established power structures and promote social change.* Activist groups and grassroots movements frequently organize in the context of technology to fight against technical injustices and promote digital rights.
- In the creation and control of technology, movements like those supporting digital rights, open-source software, and free culture advance the values of accountability, transparency, and democratic decision-making. These movements push for alternative paradigms that put social justice and group empowerment above corporate and governmental control over technology.

3.2.6. Technology and Intersectionality:

- The significance of *Intersectionality*—which studies how different social stratifications, such as race, gender, class, and ethnicity, overlap and compound to influence people's experiences and opportunities—is emphasized by conflict theory. *Intersectionality in the context of technology draws attention to the ways in which it can serve to maintain current injustices and interlocking oppressive systems.*
- For instance, biases in AI and algorithmic systems can support

socioeconomic inequalities, gender discrimination, and racial profiling. Furthermore, access and engagement in the technology industry may be restricted for marginalized groups, including women, people of colour, and low-income communities. This can exacerbate digital gaps and reinforce social hierarchies.

To sum up, conflict theory provides important insights into the technological aspects that are social, political, and economic. IT professionals can advance fair and inclusive technical solutions and gain a greater understanding of the societal effects of technology by examining power dynamics, social disparities, and resistance movements.

This viewpoint calls on IT workers to scrutinize technology's role in upholding or undermining current power systems and to push for technological advancements that advance human rights, social justice, and democratic government.

3.3. Symbolic Interactionism and the Digital Age

A sociological viewpoint known as *symbolic interactionism* places a strong emphasis on the role that symbols, meanings, and social interactions play in influencing both individual behaviours and societal processes. *Symbolic interactionism offers important insights on how technology affects social relationships, identities, and human interactions in the context of the digital age.*

Let's examine in more detail how symbolic interactionism and the digital age relate to each other:

3.3.1. Interpretation and Technology Artefacts:

- *Symbolic interactionism emphasizes how meanings and symbols influence how people behave and interact with each other in social situations.* In the era of digitalization, electronic objects like social media, virtual reality environments, and cellphones function as symbolic representations that have personal and societal importance.

- For instance, smartphones represent connectedness, convenience, and personal identity in addition to being tools for communication. Social media sites like Facebook, Instagram, and Twitter are symbolic arenas where people create and enact their social networks, connections, and identities. Users can engage with digital representations of themselves and other people in virtual reality environments, which build symbolic worlds that let them experience new realities.

3.3.2. Identity Formation in Online Communities:

- *Symbolic interactionism places emphasis on how social interactions mould people's identities and perceptions of themselves.* Online communities and platforms give people in the digital age a place to create and negotiate their identities through symbolic connections with other people.
- People can connect with like-minded people online through communities like forums, subreddits, and gaming groups. These communities allow people to share experiences and create social bonds based on common interests, identities, and values. These virtual places function as symbolic settings where people express themselves, try out various personas, and look to other people for approval and affirmation.

3.3.3. Symbolic Communication and Digital Literacy:

- *Symbolic interactionism emphasizes how crucial language and communication are in forming social reality.* Digital communication tools and platforms mediate symbolic relationships in the digital age, affecting people's self-expression, communication, and interpretation of social cues.
- Effective symbolic interaction in the digital age requires digital literacy, or the capacity to explore and assess digital information and communication tools critically. It encompasses abilities like online etiquette, media literacy, and information literacy that allow people to interact with digital environments responsibly, communicate clearly, and identify reliable sources.

3.3.4. Virtual Communities and Social Networks:

- *Symbolic interactionism emphasizes how important interpersonal connections and social networks are in influencing people's behaviour and the way society is organized.* Virtual communities and social networks, which transcend physical barriers in the digital era, allow people to connect and build relationships with people from different places and cultural backgrounds.

- Social networking sites like Facebook, LinkedIn, and Twitter give users the means to share content, voice ideas, and uphold relationships, so facilitating symbolic interactions and social connections. Through these platforms, people can curate their digital identities, make symbolic representations of themselves, and communicate with others continuously.

3.3.5. Technological Mediation of Social Interaction:

- *Symbolic interactionism acknowledges that people's perceptions, interpretations, and reactions to social cues are shaped by technology, which mediates social interactions.* The dynamics of in-person and virtual encounters are influenced by digital age technology including social networking platforms, video conferencing, and instant messaging.
- Video conferencing technologies, such as Zoom and Skype, facilitate remote interactions by simulating face-to-face communication through visual and audio signals. The quality and character of social interactions are shaped by these new affordances and obstacles, which include screen weariness, multitasking, and digital distractions.

To sum up, symbolic interactionism provides insightful understandings of how technology affects social relationships, identities, and human interactions in the digital age. IT specialists can learn more about the development of online identities and communities, the significance of technological objects for symbolic meanings, the relevance of digital literacy in communication, and how technology mediates social interaction.

From this vantage point, IT workers are encouraged to create and implement solutions that support genuine social relationships, meaningful communication, and the ability for people to navigate and engage appropriately in digital settings.

Chapter 4: The Digital Divide: Social Stratification in the Information Age

4.1. Defining the Digital Divide

The difference in access to digital technologies and the internet between those who do and do not is known as the *"Digital Divide."* It includes differences in access to digital information and services, *Hardware* (such computers, smartphones, and tablets), *Internet Connectivity* (broadband access), and *Digital Literacy* (the ability to utilize digital technologies well).

Let me examine each facet of the digital divide:

4.1.1. Access to Hardware:

- One of the main components of the digital divide is *Access to Hardware*, including computers, cellphones, and tablets. For budgetary or infrastructural reasons, many people do not have access to these gadgets, especially those living in low-income or rural areas.
- The lack of access to hardware due to the digital divide can make socioeconomic disparities worse since people without it may not be able to take advantage of internet services, career opportunities, educational materials, or other digital tools that are becoming more and more necessary in today's world.

4.1.2. Connectivity to the Internet:

- Another crucial aspect of the digital divide is *Internet Availability*, especially broadband access. Even while internet connectivity is now more widely available worldwide, there are still big differences in terms of pricing, dependability, and access speeds—especially in rural and isolated locations.
- People's capacity to participate in e-commerce, access online education, telecommute for work, obtain healthcare services

remotely, and take part in civic activities like online voting or using government services is restricted by unreliable internet connectivity.

4.1.3. **Digital Literacy:**

- The abilities, know-how, and proficiencies required to operate digital devices and surf the internet are referred to as *Digital Literacy*. This includes fundamental abilities like using word processing and spreadsheet software, browsing the internet, assessing online content, and safeguarding one's security and privacy when using computers and cellphones.
- *The elderly, the disabled, low-income persons, and those with little formal education are among the marginalized and vulnerable groups that are disproportionately impacted by the digital divide in digital literacy.* People may find it difficult to access and use digital resources and services if they lack the necessary digital literacy abilities, which will limit their ability to fully engage in the digital society.

4.1.4. **Access to Digital Services and Content:**

- *Differences in access to pertinent digital content and services can exacerbate the digital divide even in cases when people have hardware and internet connectivity.* This covers social media networks, e-government services, telemedicine platforms, e-commerce platforms, online employment sites, and educational materials.
- Online digital information and services could not necessarily be inclusive of all populations or easily accessible, further marginalizing already marginalized groups. For instance, there might not be various language versions of the content or accessibility features that prevent persons with impairments

from accessing it.

A multimodal strategy that tackles the fundamental obstacles to affordability, accessibility, and digital literacy is needed to close the digital divide. This could consist of:

- **Infrastructure Development**: includes investing in digital infrastructure to increase internet access and dependability as well as extending broadband infrastructure to underserved areas.
- **Programs for Affordability and Subsidies**: Offering financial aid or other incentives to families and individuals with low incomes so they can purchase digital gadgets and inexpensive internet services.
- **Training in Digital Skills**: Providing initiatives and programs for digital literacy to provide people the information and abilities they need to successfully traverse the digital environment.
- **Content Accessibility:** Ensuring that digital services and content are accessible to a wide range of people, including those who are non-native English speakers and people with impairments.
- **Public-Private Partnerships**: Working together with private sector companies, NGOs, and governments to create and carry out programs that support digital inclusion for all parts of society and work to close the digital gap.

In order to ensure that everyone has equal access to digital technologies and stays ahead of the curve in the digital age, it is imperative for IT professionals to support laws and programs that address the digital divide.

4.2. Socioeconomic Factors Contributing to the Digital Divide

A complex web of interrelated socioeconomic factors influences the digital divide, which is the difference in access to digital technologies and the internet between those who do and do not.

Let me discuss these elements in more detail:

technologies well). Let me examine each facet of the digital divide as an IT specialist:

4.2.1. Wealth and Income Disparities:

- The digital divide is mostly a result of *differences in wealth and income*. Due to financial limitations, lower-class individuals and families may find it difficult to purchase the essential gear (such as laptops, smartphones, and tablets) and internet connectivity.

- *Many marginalized people have financial obstacles that keep them from obtaining necessary digital tools and resources.* This limits their capacity to take full advantage of educational opportunities, participate fully in the digital economy, and participate in online civic activities.

4.2.2. Geographical Location:

- *Geographical differences, especially those between urban and rural areas, might make the digital divide worse.* Compared to urban regions, rural communities frequently have less access to broadband infrastructure and high-speed internet service.

- Internet service companies may find it too expensive to install broadband infrastructure in rural and isolated locations, leaving underprivileged populations with little access to dependable internet services. This regional discrepancy exacerbates socioeconomic inequality and further marginalizes rural inhabitants.

4.2.3. Academic Achievement:

- Access to digital technologies and digital literacy are directly related to educational success. *Higher educated people are more likely to possess the abilities, know-how, and resources needed to successfully traverse the digital environment.*
- On the other hand, people with less education might not possess the digital literacy abilities required to access and make use of digital resources and services. Due to the obstacles that people with low levels of education encounter in the digital age when it comes to work, education, and social participation, the digital skills gap exacerbates socioeconomic inequality.

4.2.4. Employment and Occupational Status:

- *The work and occupational status of an individual influence their ability to access digital technologies and internet connectivity. White-collar professionals with advanced skills might have easier access to digital tools and resources at work.*
- On the other hand, people with low-skilled, blue-collar professions or those with unstable employment could not have access to digital devices and dependable internet connectivity, which would restrict their capacity to take advantage of online job postings, engage in remote work, and obtain educational materials.

4.2.5. Demographic Factors:

- *Access to digital technology can be influenced by the intersection of socioeconomic status and demographic characteristics, including age, race, ethnicity, and language.* Language hurdles, cultural disparities, and generational gaps may present additional obstacles to digital inclusion for older persons, members of racial and ethnic minorities, and non-native language speakers.
- In comparison to younger generations, *older persons might, for instance, have lower levels of digital literacy and feel less at ease utilizing digital technology,* which would restrict their access to online information and services.

4.2.6. Policy Environment and Digital Infrastructure:

- *The regulatory framework governing technology deployment and access, along with the availability and quality of digital infrastructure, can have an impact on the digital divide.* Inequalities in access to digital technologies can be made worse by underinvesting in broadband infrastructure, deregulating the telecoms industry, and not providing government subsidies or incentives for digital inclusion.
- To address the socioeconomic reasons that lead to digital inequality, government policies and efforts that promote digital literacy, improve broadband access, and bridge the digital divide are crucial.

To sum up. To tackle the socioeconomic reasons that contribute to the digital divide, a comprehensive approach is necessary, addressing systemic inequities, affordability restrictions, gaps in digital literacy, and hurdles to access. Targeted interventions including financial aid for low-income households, broadband infrastructure investments in underserved areas, digital skills training programs, and legislative measures that support digital inclusion and equity for all parts of society could fall under this category.

Promoting laws and programs that take these socioeconomic aspects into account is crucial for IT professionals in order to close the digital gap and ensure that everyone has fair access to digital technologies.

4.3. Implications of the Digital Divide for Society

The difference between people who have access to digital technologies and the internet and those who do not is known as the "digital divide," and it has a significant impact on society.

Let's examine these consequences in more detail:

4.3.1. Increasing Socioeconomic Inequalities:

- *The digital divide's aggravation of pre-existing social inequality is arguably its most important consequence.* Being able to use digital technology and the internet has become more and more necessary for people to participate in modern society. This includes being able to access government services, healthcare, employment prospects, and educational materials.
- Comparing those without access to digital technologies to those with digital connections puts the former at a considerable disadvantage. Due to limited prospects for upward mobility and the reinforcement of pre-existing inequalities based on income, education, geography, and other factors, this may prolong socioeconomic inequities.

4.3.2. Restricted Opportunities for Education and Learning:

- The digital gap has a significant impact on learning and education. *Lack of access to digital technology or dependable internet connectivity might make it difficult for students to use educational resources, engage in online learning environments, or finish tasks that call for the internet.*
- This can exacerbate academic success disparities and impede

educational attainment by creating larger educational gaps between kids who have access to digital devices and those who do not. Furthermore, the COVID-19 pandemic's impact on the shift to digital learning modalities has brought attention to how urgent it is to close the digital divide in order to guarantee that all students have equitable access to education.

4.3.3. Barriers to Financial Prospects:

- *Digital technology access is becoming more and more necessary to take advantage of economic opportunities, engage in the digital economy, and find work.* People who don't have access to digital tools and internet connectivity could find it difficult to use online job portals, find employment, or take advantage of remote work opportunities.
- The digital gap can contribute to economic marginalization and the perpetuation of poverty cycles by prolonging unemployment and underemployment among disadvantaged communities. Ensuring that everyone has access to the economic opportunities provided by digital technologies and fostering economic inclusion require bridging the digital divide.

4.3.4. Restricted Access to Medical Services:

- *Access to telehealth platforms, digital health records, remote monitoring tools, and online health resources has increased as a result of the digitization of healthcare services.* Those without access to digital technology or dependable internet connectivity, however, might find it difficult to use these services.
- Inequalities in healthcare outcomes and access can be made worse by the digital gap, especially for marginalized and

vulnerable groups. Ensuring fair access to healthcare services and advancing health equity for all members of society require addressing the digital divide.

4.3.5. Civic Engagement and Digital Citizenship:

- *Digital technology access is necessary to engage in democratic activities including voting, advocacy, and community organization, as well as to access government services and participate in civic life.* People who lack internet connectivity or digital technologies may be denied the right to vote and prevented from fully engaging in civic life.
- Promoting digital citizenship and making sure that everyone has the means to participate in democratic processes, access government services, and engage in civic activities require closing the digital divide.

4.3.6. Social Marginalization and Isolation:

- *Social exclusion and isolation can be exacerbated by the digital gap, especially for the elderly, the disabled, and other vulnerable groups.* People might not be able to engage in social networks, communicate with friends and family, or access online support groups if they do not have access to digital technologies or dependable internet connectivity.
- In order to combat social isolation and promote social inclusion, it is imperative that the digital gap be addressed. This will guarantee that every member of society has the ability to engage in social interactions, connect with others, and access support networks.

To sum up, the digital gap has a significant impact on society. It exacerbates social injustices, restricts access to healthcare services, limits political engagement, and makes it harder for people to pursue economic and educational opportunities. A comprehensive strategy that tackles access obstacles, affordability limitations, gaps in digital literacy, and systematic injustices is needed to close the digital divide.

In order to guarantee that everyone in society has access to the advantages provided by digital technologies, it is imperative for IT professionals to support laws and programs that advance digital inclusion and equity.

Chapter 5: Social Networks and Online Communities

5.1. The Rise of Social Networking Platforms

The emergence of social networking platforms has completely changed how individuals connect, communicate, and engage with each other in both online and offline settings.

Let me explore the several facets of this phenomenon:

5.1.1. Social Networking Platform Evolution:

- *The social media landscape has changed dramatically since the internet's inception.* Although the idea of online social networks originated in the 1990s with sites like Friendster and Six Degrees, the emergence of sites like Facebook, LinkedIn, and MySpace in the middle of the 2000s signalled a shift in the acceptance and prevalence of social networking.
- Social networking sites have evolved since then to accommodate a wider range of users, interests, and demographics. There are now platforms like TikTok, Instagram, Snapchat, Twitter, and more that each provide something different.

5.1.2. Global Access and Interconnectivity:

- *Social media networks have brought billions of people together globally, bridging geographic and cultural divides.* Regardless of where they are in the world, these platforms give people a place to connect with friends, family, acquaintances, and people who share their interests.
- Social networking sites' worldwide reach has made it easier for people to communicate, collaborate, and share information across cultural boundaries, strengthening the sense of

interconnection and global community.

5.1.3. Interaction and Communication:

- *Social networking sites act as central centres for communication, allowing users to share multimedia content, have conversations in real time, and send messages.* User involvement and engagement are facilitated by features like direct messaging, shares, likes, and comments.
- Social networking sites have transformed communication by enhancing its accessibility, instantaneity, and interactivity. They give people a platform to connect with others in ways that were previously impossible, express themselves, and share their ideas and experiences.

5.1.4. Building One's Identity and Personal Brand:

- *Through the use of social networking sites, people may construct and project their identities online, influencing how others see them.* Users can develop personal brands, post images and videos, highlight their skills and interests, and establish profiles.
- Professional networking and career growth are catered to by platforms such as LinkedIn, which allow users to highlight their accomplishments, credentials, and talents. Other social media sites, such as Instagram and TikTok, let users express themselves visually and creatively while showcasing their individuality and inventiveness.

5.1.5. Establishing and Fostering Community:

- *Social networking sites make it easier for online groups based on identities, affiliations, or common interests to emerge. Through* forums, hashtags, groups, and pages, users can interact with people who have similar interests, passions, or worldviews.

- Social networking platforms' online communities have a variety of uses, from promoting solidarity and support to planning events, energizing social movements, and encouraging group action. These communities support group empowerment, identity building, and social cohesiveness.

5.1.6. Data Security and Privacy Issues:

- *With the popularity of social networking sites, people are becoming more concerned about security, privacy, and the use of user data for partisan or commercial gain.* Data breaches, illegal access, and improper use of user data have brought attention to the necessity of strong security and privacy measures.
- Social networking sites gather a tonne of user data, which can be made money with data analytics, targeted advertising, and profiling. This data includes browsing patterns, personal information, and social interactions.
- For social networking companies and authorities, striking a balance between the advantages of individualized services and the defence of user privacy continues to be a major concern.

5.1.7. Effects on Culture and Society:

- *Social conventions, interpersonal connections, and cultural practices have all been impacted by social networking platforms, which have had a significant impact on society and culture. They* have changed how people establish and nurture connections, seek approval from others, and build friendships.
- The emergence of social networking sites has also changed news consumption patterns, entertainment tastes, and media consumption behaviours.

- Many users now rely mostly on social media sites like Facebook and Twitter for news and information, which shapes public opinion and the conversation around social and political concerns.

To sum up, the emergence of social networking sites has completely changed how people connect, communicate, and engage with one other in the digital age. These platforms have changed how people communicate, made the world more connected, made it easier to build one's identity and personal brand, promoted online communities, sparked worries about data security and privacy, and changed cultural norms.

In order to navigate the intricacies of social networking platforms and maximize their potential for positive social impact, IT experts must have a thorough awareness of the technological, social, and cultural ramifications of these platforms.

5.2. Identity Formation in Online Spaces

The process of forming an identity in virtual environments is complex and influenced by various factors such as personal choice, social connections, available technology, and cultural settings.

Let's examine the many facets of identity building in online environments from the perspective of an IT specialist:

5.2.1. Digital Demonstration of Self:

- *People can create and display digital identities on online platforms that may be different from their offline personas.* Users have the ability to post material that reflects their values, interests, and aspirations, as well as customize their profiles and choose profile images.

- Strategic choices regarding what to share and how to display oneself online are part of digital self-presentation, and they can affect how others view and engage with the individual. Identity performance, impression management, and selective self-disclosure may all be a part of this process.

5.2.2. Pseudonym and Anonymity:

- *Users can interact with people in online spaces without disclosing their true identity thanks to the many levels of anonymity and pseudonymity that these venues offer.* Participating in delicate or stigmatized conversations, experimenting with various personas, and unrestrained self-expression can all be made easier by anonymity.

- But anonymity also creates issues with accountability, trust, and authenticity since people can act in a damaging or dishonest way without worrying about the consequences. By using aliases or handles in place of real names, pseudonymous identities provide a middle ground between anonymity and accountability, allowing people to create online personas while yet retaining some degree of privacy.

5.2.3. Digital Traces and Enduring Effects:

- *People leave digital footprints, or traces, of their activities and conversations since online interactions are digital in nature.* These digital traces may consist of search history, online transactions, likes, shares, comments, and postings on social media.
- Online conversations can be recorded, saved, and shared indefinitely, in contrast to real encounters, which might be fleeting or forgotten over time. The enduring nature of digital footprints bears significance for identity and reputation management, since an individual's past conduct and demeanour may persist in moulding their future perceptions.

5.2.4. Internet Groups and Partnerships:

- *Because they give people a place to connect with like-minded people, exchange stories, and reinforce their identities, online communities are essential to the construction of identity.* These groups could be founded on common passions, identities, affiliations, or interests.
- Participating in virtual communities can impact people's feeling of acceptance, self-worth, and personal growth.
- People can strengthen aspects of their identities and gain a feeling of community by taking part in discussions, sharing their experiences, and getting support and affirmation from others.

5.2.5. Critical Engagement and Digital Literacy:

- *Proficiency in digital literacy is crucial for effectively navigating virtual environments and critically interacting with digital content and platforms.* To preserve their privacy, assess the reliability of online material, and participate in positive online conversation, people must acquire skills like media literacy, information literacy, and online safety.

- Questioning presumptions, confronting prejudices, and being aware of the possible effects of one's online activity on oneself and others are all part of critical engagement with online content and interactions. This entails being informed about the dangers of false information, echo chambers, cyberbullying, and online abuse.

5.2.6. Online Identities and Intersectionality:

- *Numerous intersecting elements, such as age, social class, geography, race, gender, sexual orientation, and ethnicity, shape online identities.* People's experiences, perceptions, and interactions in online settings are influenced by these intersecting identities.

- The concept of intersectionality emphasizes how crucial it is to acknowledge the diversity and complexity of online identities as well as how various facets of identity interact to influence people's online experiences. Online platforms can encourage inclusivity, diversity, and equity in their practices, policy, and design by recognizing intersectionality.

To sum up, the process of forming an identity in virtual places is intricate and ever-changing, influenced by a range of factors such as personal preferences, social interactions, available technology, and cultural background. Online platforms give people the chance to express themselves, connect with others, and explore their identities, but they also bring up issues with digital literacy, privacy, anonymity, and authenticity.

IT professionals must comprehend the subtleties of identity formation in online contexts in order to create digital environments that are empowering, inclusive, and ethical while also promoting people's identity development and well-being.

5.3. Community Dynamics in Virtual Environments

Online communities and digital places give rise to patterns of interaction, social relationships, and collective behaviors known as *Community Dynamics*. Numerous elements, such as the virtual environment's architecture, the traits of its members, and the customs and conventions that regulate interactions inside the community, all have an impact on these dynamics.

Let me discuss the main facets of community dynamics in virtual environments from the perspective of an IT specialist:

1. **Similar Interests and Objectives:**

    - *Virtual communities frequently emerge around common passions, pastimes, or objectives.* Whether it's a professional network for people in a certain field, a subreddit for a specialized pastime, or a forum for video game aficionados, mutual interests give community members a place to connect.
    - The degree of participation, cohesiveness, and cooperation within a community can be shaped by the strength of common interests and objectives. Members are more likely to actively participate in and contribute to conversations and activities if they have a strong interest in the topic of the community.

1. **Social Codes of Conduct:**

    - *Similar to physical communities, virtual communities have their own codes of conduct, social standards, and regulations that dictate appropriate conduct and interactions.* These standards may be outlined clearly by administrators or moderators of the community or they may develop naturally via interactions among members.

- Social norms in virtual settings might include standards for civil discourse, prohibitions on harassment and trolling, expectations about content sharing and self-promotion, and expectations for making constructive contributions to the community. Maintaining a welcoming and positive community atmosphere is facilitated by upholding these standards.

1. **Governance and Leadership:**

- *Governance and leadership structures are common in virtual communities to help with community management and decision-making.* Setting the tone for interactions, settling problems, and forming community dynamics are all important tasks performed by administrators, moderators, and leaders.
- Fostering a feeling of community, promoting meaningful relationships, and making sure that laws and conventions are followed are all components of effective community leadership. In addition, leaders can monitor conversations, organize community activities, and offer members of the community advice and assistance.

1. **Interaction Patterns and Communication:**

- *Depending on the platform, medium, and goal of the community, there are different patterns of communication and engagement within virtual communities.* While some groups may include multimedia content like photos, videos, or live streams, others may predominantly rely on text-based communication through forums, chat rooms, or messaging apps.
- There can be variations in the frequency, depth, and formality of interaction patterns. While some communities value in-

depth conversations or group projects, others might have lively, fast-paced discussions. Fostering meaningful relationships requires an understanding of community members' communication habits and preferences.

1. Diversity and Inclusivity:

- *Diverse viewpoints, experiences, and backgrounds are welcomed in inclusive virtual communities.* Accepting variety makes communal interactions more vibrant, encourages innovation and creativity, and advances respect and understanding amongst people.
- The level of diversity and inclusivity within a community affects its dynamics. Dynamic and lively communities are those that actively foster diversity, confront prejudice and stereotyping, and offer safe havens for underrepresented voices.

1. Traditions and Community Rituals:

- *Virtual communities frequently establish customs, rituals, and regular gatherings that cement relationships between members and provide a feeling of community.* Weekly gatherings, talks with a specific theme, online celebrations, or group projects are a few examples of these rituals.
- Engaging in customs and rituals within the community fosters social bonds, strengthens community identity, and gives people a chance to add to the community's overall experience. These customs frequently have a major influence on how communities interact and stay cohesive throughout time.

In summary, a complex interaction between common interests, social norms, leadership roles, communication styles, inclusion initiatives, and community rituals shapes community dynamics in virtual settings. For IT professionals to create and oversee virtual communities that promote community objectives, encourage meaningful interactions, and offer great experiences to its members, they must have a thorough awareness of these dynamics.

It is possible to enable communities to flourish and reach their full potential in the digital age by utilizing technology to build inclusive and stimulating virtual spaces.

Chapter 6: Work and Employment in the Digital Era

6.1. Automation and Its Impact on Employment

Automation, or *the use of technology to carry out tasks without the need for human intervention,* has revolutionized a number of industries. Efficiency, productivity, and economic growth have all increased as a result of it, but employment dynamics have also changed significantly.

Automation technologies are those made to substitute machine labour for human labour in certain kinds of economic processes. The effect of new technologies on the workplace has received a lot of attention lately. Automation technologies, such artificial intelligence and industrial robots, have advanced significantly over the past 20 years, making it possible to conduct non-routine jobs that were previously thought to be exclusively performed by labour.

Automation technologies have the potential to replace humans in a wide range of occupations, both high- and low-skilled ones, and many of these workers may lose their jobs in the future. Numerous studies measuring the impact of automation technologies at different levels of study have emerged due to the relevance of the topic and the scale of their impact.

Here, we examine the idea of automation, its various forms, and the complex effects it has on labour.

6.1.1. Types of Automation:

1. Industrial Automation:

- **Example:** For instance, robotic arms used in production.
- **Impact:** Lowers expenses, minimizes errors, and boosts manufacturing efficiency. However, it may result in those who perform manual labour losing their jobs.

1. **Software Automating:**

- **Example:** One instance is the use of robotic process automation (RPA) for office work.
- **Impact:** Automates repetitive digital chores such as processing invoices, entering data, and answering customer support queries. In addition to creating new opportunities for IT professionals who administer and maintain these systems, it can lessen the need for human labour in these areas.

1. **Machine Learning (ML) And Artificial Intelligence (AI):**

- **Example:** Include chatbots in customer service and predictive analytics in banking.
- **Impact:** Large-scale data analysis and insight-gathering, intricate task execution, and consumer interaction are all possible with AI and ML. They improve operational effectiveness and decision-making, but they might take the place of positions involving data analysis, assistance, and specific decision-making procedures.

1. **Autonomous Systems:**

- **Example:** Drones and self-driving cars are two examples.
- **Impact:** By lowering the need for human drivers, it has the potential to completely transform the logistics and transportation industries. On the other hand, this can result in a large loss of jobs in these sectors while also generating new jobs in the creation, supervision, and upkeep of autonomous technologies.

6.1.2. Impact on Employment
6.1.2.1. Positive Impacts:

1. **Job Creation in New Sectors:**

- **Example:** An illustration would be the growth of the IT sector and the resulting demand for AI experts, data scientists, and software engineers.
- **Justification:** New job categories are frequently created as a result of automation. For example, as AI technology advances, there is a greater need for machine learning engineers, data analysts, and AI ethicists.

1. **Enhanced Efficiency and Economic Development:**

- **Example:** An example would be productivity-boosting automated manufacturing techniques.
- **Justification:** Automation boosts productivity and lowers expenses, which could result in lower consumer prices and increased output, both of which support economic growth.

1. **Enhanced Quality of Work:**

- **Example:** One example would be the automation of risky construction or mining operations.
- **Explanation:** Automation can increase workplace safety and lower the risk of harm by taking over physically taxing and hazardous occupations, freeing up workers to perform more important and low-risk tasks.

6.1.2.2. Adverse Negative Impacts:

1. **Loss of Employment:**

- **Example:** Self-checkout machines have supplanted cashiers in retail establishments.

- **Justification:** Automation threatens a lot of repetitive and routine employment, which will result in job losses in industries including manufacturing, retail, and administration.

1. **Skill Gaps and Inequality:**

- **Example:** An illustration would be workers in conventional sectors who are having trouble finding new jobs in tech-driven markets.
- **Justification:** The demands of the newly created employment brought about by automation frequently do not align with the skills of the workers who are being replaced. Economic disparity and income inequality may rise as a result of this.

1. **Social and Economic Disruptions:**

- **Example:** The economic impact of factory automation is being felt by entire towns that depend on manufacturing jobs.
- **Justification:** Prolonged job displacement can have a knock-on effect that impacts individuals individually as well as their families and communities, creating more significant social and economic problems.

6.1.3. Addressing the Challenges:

Several tactics can be used to lessen automation's detrimental effects:

1. **Upskilling and Reskilling:**

- **Examples** include business and governmental training initiatives that emphasize digital skills.

- **Justification:** It's critical to offer people the education and training they need to adapt to new positions in the changing labour market. Programs like online classes, coding boot camps, and vocational training can assist employees in learning new skills.

1. **Supportive Policies:**

- **Example:** Include job placement assistance and unemployment compensation.
- **Justification:** Policies that assist employees in transitions can be put in place by governments. Examples of these include increasing unemployment benefits, providing job placement assistance, and pressuring businesses to make workforce development investments.

1. **Promoting Inclusive Growth:**

- **Example:** Promoting diverse recruiting procedures in tech organizations is one example.
- **Justification:** In order to guarantee that the advantages of automation are broadly shared, inclusive growth strategies are needed. This entails encouraging diversity in the IT industry, lending a hand to small and medium-sized businesses, and making investments in underprivileged areas.

In summary, Automation surely alters the nature of work in significant ways. Although it presents chances for higher output and the creation of new jobs, it also brings with it serious difficulties like skill mismatches and job displacement. Societies can more effectively negotiate the shift to an automated future by proactively addressing these issues through inclusive growth strategies, regulations that support it, and reskilling initiatives.

6.2. Remote Work: Opportunities and Challenges

Thanks to developments in information technology, *remote work has grown in popularity*, particularly after the COVID-19 epidemic. Employers and employees alike can benefit much from it, but there are also a number of issues that must be resolved for it to be successful.

By the end of March 2020, *governments all over the world had made the decision to impose restrictions on population movement in an effort to slow the spread of Covid-19 and limit the number of individuals to whom an infected person can transmit the virus.* Due to these lockdowns, "non-essential" firms had to temporarily close, forcing millions of individuals to work from home. Numerous nations experienced the closure of establishments like childcare centers, colleges, businesses, dental offices, and public spaces like cafes and restaurants. Millions of workers have been compelled by this lockdown to accept remote employment whenever it is feasible, making working from home a necessity rather than a choice.

In order to understand the dynamics of implementing, embedding, and integrating new technologies and practices into businesses, organizations were forced by COVID-19 to adopt online working from home practices in a big way. They do this by drawing on the Normalization Process Theory (NPT) and its underlying components. Even while working remotely with online technology has numerous benefits, there are drawbacks and hazards associated with working from home, including uneven job overload and deadline demands that can negatively impact health and welfare.

Here, we go into the specifics of working remotely, examining its advantages and drawbacks using real-world instances.

6.2.1. Possibilities for Remote Work:

1. **Greater Flexibility:**

- **Example:** For instance, workers are able to work from coffee shops, co-working facilities, or their homes.
- **Justification:** Employees that work remotely have more freedom to select their workspace, which promotes a better work-life balance. This adaptability can lessen burnout and improve job satisfaction.

1. **Getting into the World's Talent Pool:**

- **Example:** For instance, a Silicon Valley software company is employing an Indian developer.
- **Explanation:** Employers can now choose from a global pool of talented applicants rather than just local ones. This variety may inspire creative solutions and thoughts.

1. **Savings On Costs:**

- **Example:** For instance, less huge office premises are required.
- **Reason:** Employers can cut expenses on fixed costs like utilities, rent, and office supplies. Workers can also cut costs on their transportation expenses and business apparel.

1. **Increased Productivity:**

- **Example:** For instance, studies reveal that remote workers frequently put in more hours.
- **Explanation:** Working remotely allows employees to be more productive because there are fewer outside distractions and travel time to the office. Effective remote collaboration is facilitated by programs like Zoom, Trello, and Slack.

1. **Advantages for the Environment:**

- **Example:** Lower carbon emissions as a result of fewer commuting hours.
- **Justification:** Since fewer workers commute, there is less traffic and a decrease in greenhouse gas emissions, remote work can help reduce carbon footprints.

6.2.2. Problems with Remote Work:

1. **Collaboration and Communication:**

- **Example:** Inadequate face-to-face interaction leading to miscommunication.
- **Explanation:** Collaboration and efficient communication can be difficult for remote teams. In virtual meetings, nonverbal cues are lost, and synchronous communication may become more difficult due to time zone variations.

1. **Being Alone and Isolated:**

- **Example:** Employees who work remotely are losing out on social opportunities with co-workers.
- **Justification:** Feelings of loneliness and isolation brought on by remote work might have a detrimental effect on one's mental health and level of job satisfaction in general. Workers lose out on opportunities for networking and casual discussions.

1. **Work-Life Balance:**

- **Example:** Finding it difficult to keep business and personal life apart.

- **Justification:** In the absence of defined boundaries, remote workers may find it difficult to put in their workdays, which could result in extended hours and even burnout. The boundaries between one's personal and professional lives might become hazy in the home.

1. **Privacy and Security Concerns:**

- **Example:** Remote access increases the danger of data breaches.
- **Explanation:** If appropriate safeguards are not taken, remote work may expose businesses to cybersecurity dangers. It is essential to use VPNs, make sure connections are secure, and warn staff members about phishing scams.

1. **Monitoring and Managing Performance:**

- **Example:** Difficulties in monitoring output.
- **Justification:** It could be challenging for managers to properly track and assess the work of distant workers. It's possible that traditional productivity measures don't apply, in which case trust becomes essential.

6.2.3. Overcoming the Obstacles:

1. **Effective Communication Tools:**

- **Example:** Using Zoom for video conferences with Slack for real-time communications is one example.
- **Justification:** Cooperation can be improved by putting in place strong communication tools and defining explicit communication guidelines. Consistent virtual gatherings and check-ins can support the upkeep of team cohesiveness.

1. **Building a Robust Corporate Culture:**

- **Example:** Examples include online social gatherings and virtual team-building exercises.
- **Justification:** Providing chances for interpersonal communication and group cohesion in an online setting can help reduce feelings of loneliness. Relationships can be strengthened by promoting casual talks through happy hours or virtual coffee breaks.

1. **Setting Clear Boundaries:**

- **Example:** Designating particular workstations and hours of operation.
- **Justification:** It's critical to assist workers in drawing distinct lines between their personal and professional lives. A healthier work-life balance can be supported by encouraging regular breaks and the use of separate workspaces at home.

1. **Improving Cybersecurity:**

- **Example:** For instance, requiring frequent security training and multi-factor authentication.
- **Justification:** It's critical to put solid cybersecurity measures into place. Company data can be safeguarded by utilizing encryption, giving personnel secure devices, and carrying out frequent security audits.

1. **Trust and Performance Metrics:**

- **Example:** Paying more attention to outcomes than two hours done.
- **Justification:** Using outcome-based performance

measurements can help provide a more accurate picture of output. Establishing a culture of trust and responsibility makes sure that workers are inspired to perform at the highest level and feel empowered.

In summary, many benefits come with working remotely, such as more freedom, cost savings, and access to a worldwide talent pool. But it also brings with it difficulties like isolation, communication obstacles, and cybersecurity threats. Organizations can effectively navigate the complexities of remote work, maximizing its benefits while mitigating its drawbacks, by utilizing efficient communication tools, cultivating a strong company culture, setting clear boundaries, improving cybersecurity, and putting a strong emphasis on results-based performance metrics.

6.3. Gig Economy and Precarious Labour in the Digital Age

With the introduction of digital platforms, the gig economy—which is defined by temporary, flexible, and independent labour—has experienced tremendous growth. Although it presents chances for flexible work and income generating, it also brings with it issues with worker rights and job security.

When we examine the various terms that are used in this field of *Gig Economy*, we realise that "online labour" is the most important term from the perspective of work and labour; "online outsourcing" is the most important term from the perspective of clients; and "(digital) gig economy" is the most important term overall. Online labour is described as *contingent (task- or project-based) intangible work that is performed digitally and paid for through online outsourcing platforms, which function as marketplaces connecting buyers and sellers.*

In the digital age, the gig economy and remote employment have changed dramatically, affecting the rights, well-being, and financial security of workers. Here, we examine unstable work and the gig economy, showing its advantages and drawbacks with pertinent instances.

6.3.1. **Comprehending The Gig Economy**: The phrase "gig economy" describes a labour market where freelance or contract work predominates over full-time employment. By matching workers with gigs, digital platforms like as TaskRabbit, Upwork, and Uber have contributed to the rise of this sector.

- **Examples:**

1. **Uber and Lyft:** Examples of platforms used by drivers to offer

ride-hailing services are Uber and Lyft.

2. **TaskRabbit:** Independent contractors provide a range of services, such as moving, cleaning, and home repair.

3. **Upwork and Fiverr**: Experts offer services including writing, graphic design, and programming on Upwork and Fiverr.

6.3.2. Opportunities in the Gig Economy:

1. **Flexibility:**
   - **Example: An illustration of this would be a graphic designer selecting tasks based on scheduling.**
   - **Explanation: The option to choose when and where they work gives gig workers the flexibility to pursue different hobbies or commitments and a better work-life balance.**

2. **Getting into a Larger Market:**
   - **Example: For instance, a freelance writer on Upwork can collaborate with international clients.**
   - **Explanation: The explanation is that workers have access to a worldwide customer base through digital platforms, which expands their market and revenue prospects.**

3. **Extra Revenue:**
   - **Example: An example might be a full-time teacher who works weekends as an Uber driver.**
   - **Justification: Having a side gig can help people reach their financial objectives and manage economic instability by bringing in extra revenue.**

4. **Low Entry Barrier:**
   - **Example: For instance, anyone with a car can begin providing rides for ride-sharing companies.**

- ○ **Justification: People can start making money right away without requiring a lot of capital or qualifications thanks to the low entry requirements of many gig platforms.**

6.3.3. Difficulties and Precarious Work:

1. No Job Security:

- **Example:** A driver for Uber who notices changes in customer demand.
- **Justification:** There is no assurance of consistent work or long-term employment for gig workers, and their earnings are frequently erratic and unpredictable.

1. Lack of Advantages

- **Example:** For instance, Fiverr freelancers are not eligible for retirement or health insurance.
- **Justification:** Gig workers often have less financial security than regular employees since they do not receive benefits like health insurance, paid time off, or retirement contributions.

1. Uncertainty in Legal Protections:

- **Case in point:** legal disputes regarding the employment status of Uber drivers versus independent contractors.
- **Justification:** Gig workers' legal status is frequently unclear, which gives rise to disagreements regarding rights and protections. The fact that many gig workers are categorized as independent contractors restricts their access to labour laws and benefits.

1. **The Volatility of Income:**

- **Example:** Variations in seasonal demand have an impact on delivery drivers' earnings.
- **Explanation:** Due to the great variability of earnings in the gig economy, which is influenced by competition, market demand, and platform policies, workers may experience financial instability.

1. **Isolation and Absence of Group Negotiation:**

- **Example:** Independent contractors without a unifying voice on remote job sites such as Upwork.
- **Reason:** Because they are unable to form a union or work in isolation, gig workers have less negotiating leverage and are unable to agree on improved terms or working conditions.

6.3.4. Addressing the Challenges

1. **Policy Interventions:**

- **Example:** Laws intended to reclassify gig workers as employees, such as California's AB5.
- **Justification:** Governments have the power to enact laws that guarantee gig workers the rights to health insurance, minimum wages, and unionization.

1. **Platform Accountability:**

- **Example:** As an illustration, consider platform initiatives to offer financial planning services or health insurance options.
- **Justification:** Gig economy platforms have the capacity to proactively assist their employees by providing tools, training,

and benefits that improve job security and financial stability.

1. **Group Negotiation and Advocacy:**

- **Example:** Establishing unions or groups for gig workers.
- **Justification:** Gig workers have the ability to organize into associations in order to collectively bargain for better terms, stand up for their rights, and establish support systems for one another.

1. **Education and Financial Planning:**

- **Example:** Giving gig workers resources to manage their variable revenue is one example.
- **Justification:** Teaching gig workers about investments, savings, and financial planning will help them prepare for the future and manage their fluctuating income.

In summary, the gig economy, which uses digital platforms to link workers with a worldwide market, presents substantial prospects for flexible, varied, and additional income. It does, however, also come with drawbacks, such as a lack of benefits, legal safeguards, and work stability, all of which add to the insecure labour conditions. To guarantee a just and long-lasting gig economy, lawmakers, platform providers, and employees themselves must work together to address these issues. By striking a balance between security and rights and flexibility, the gig economy can develop into a more egalitarian part of the contemporary labour market.

Chapter 7: Education and Learning in the Digital Age

7.1. Technology in the Classroom: Enhancing Learning Experiences

Technology has completely changed the classroom, improving student learning and changing conventional teaching strategies. Compared to traditional teaching approaches, instructors are increasingly using technology in the classroom to better engage students with the course material as it becomes more widely available to them.

Though researchers have been attempting to determine the most effective ways to use technology in the classroom, *there have been certain gaps in their understanding of how to integrate mobile devices*, for example, into instruction. The term "mobile learning" (M-learning) or "technology in the classroom" describes the usage of educational software on tablets, laptops, phones, and desktop computers. Since students can respond to questions and provide answers instantaneously, these technology tools enable real-time engagement between teachers and students.

Instructors can also address issues that students find challenging or address any misconceptions before going on to the next one. Thus, *educators can enhance the learning experience of their students by incorporating technology applications into live lectures*. Let's examine how different technology tools and approaches are employed in education, their advantages, and real-world applications from the perspective of an IT specialist.

7.1.1. Advantages of Technology in the Classroom:

1. **Personalized Learning:**

    - **Example:** One example would be adaptive learning websites such as Khan Academy and DreamBox.
    - **Explanation:** These platforms offer a personalized learning

experience that accommodates different demands and learning speeds by using algorithms to modify the difficulty of activities based on the student's performance.

1. **Interactive and Engaging Learning:**

- **Example:** Examples include gamified learning apps and interactive whiteboards.
- **Justification:** Resources such as SMART Boards and applications like Kahoot! enhance the interactiveness and engagement of instruction, utilizing games and multimedia to grab students' interest and make learning enjoyable.

1. **Possessing an Abundance of Knowledge:**

- **Example:** Academic journals, e-books, and online databases are a few examples.
- **Justification:** Students' knowledge base extends beyond textbooks and their research skills are improved by the abundance of material and resources they have access to online.

1. **Working Together and Communicating:**

- **Example:** Microsoft Teams and Google Classroom are two examples.
- **Justification:** These platforms make it easier for students to collaborate and communicate with one another as well as with teachers. A connected learning environment can be facilitated by features like discussion boards, document sharing, and video conferencing.

1. **Growth of Digital Capabilities:**

- **Example:** include robotics kits like LEGO Mindstorms and coding applications like Scratch.
- **Justification:** Including technology in the curriculum aids in the development of critical digital literacy abilities in the pupils. Students who engage with robotics or learn to code are better prepared for careers in the tech industry.

1. **Adaptability and Availability:**

- **Example:** Learning management systems (LMS) and online courses are two examples.
- **Justification:** Students may access course materials and turn in assignments at any time and from any location thanks to technology, which also makes flexible learning alternatives possible. Students with special needs or those who need a more flexible timetable may especially benefit from this.

7.1.2. Examples of Technology Enhancing Experience:

1. **Augmented Reality (AR) And Virtual Reality (VR):**

- **Example:** Google Expeditions and Nearpod are two examples.
- **Justification:** Immersion-based learning is made possible by VR and AR. Google Expeditions, for example, makes it feasible for students to participate in virtual field trips to historical locations, deep oceans, or even space, offering experiential learning that would not be feasible otherwise.

1. **AI Tutors (Artificial Intelligence):**

- **Example:** For instance, AI-driven technologies such as Squirrel AI.

- **Justification:** AI tutors are able to offer pupils individualized support and feedback. To optimize the learning experience, they examine student performance data to provide individualized help and pinpoint areas in which students require development.

1. **Model of the Flipped Classroom:**

- **Example:** As an illustration, consider watching lectures on YouTube or TED-Ed.
- **Justification:** In a flipped classroom, students participate in interactive activities in the classroom while watching video lectures at home. With this technique, students can learn more practically and make greater use of class time for group projects and debates.

1. **Gamification with Educational Apps:**

- **Example:** Examples include apps like Prodigy for arithmetic and Duolingo for language learning.
- **Justification:** To motivate and engage pupils, gamification in education employs elements of game design. Apps like Prodigy transform arithmetic practice into an adventure game, and Duolingo uses levels, points, and awards to make language learning fun and efficient.

1. **Online Resources for Collaboration:**

- **Example:** Padlet and Google Docs, for instance.
- **Justification:** These tools make it possible to collaborate in real time on papers and projects. With Google Docs, students may collaborate and work as a team on the same document at the same time. Students can publish multimedia, links, and

comments to Padlet, which functions as an online bulletin board.

1. **Assistive Technology:**

- **Example:** Software for text-to-speech and voice-to-text programs like Dragon NaturallySpeaking are two examples.
- **Justification:** Students with impairments are supported by assistive technology. Text-to-speech software reads text aloud to visually impaired pupils, and speech-to-text technologies translate spoken words into text to help students who struggle with writing.

7.1.3. Challenges and Considerations:

1. **Digital Divide:**

- **Justification:** Not every student has the same level of access to the internet and technology. By providing the required resources and making sure all kids can take advantage of technological improvements, schools need to close this achievement gap.

1. **Training of Teachers:**

- **Justification:** Teachers must be adept at using these technologies in order for technology integration to be effective. It takes professional development and continuous training to provide instructors the tools they need to use technology efficiently.

1. **Security and Privacy:**

- **Justification:** Maintaining student privacy and safeguarding data is essential in light of the growing usage of digital tools. Strong security measures must be put in place, and kids must learn about digital citizenship.

1. **Maintaining Equilibrium Time Spent On Screen:**

- **Justification:** Although technology has numerous advantages, spending too much time in front of a screen can be harmful. It's crucial to strike a balance between online and offline learning activities and to make sure that kids participate in both social and physical activities.

In summary, because technology in the classroom offers individualized, interactive, and easily accessible instruction, it has the potential to greatly improve student learning outcomes. With VR field trips and AI tutors, the options are endless. But in order to fully reap these rewards, issues like teacher preparation, privacy, and the digital gap must be addressed. Technology may be carefully incorporated into education to provide rich learning environments that better prepare students for the future.

7.2. Online Education: Access and Equity Considerations

With the advent of technology and the COVID-19 epidemic, online education has grown in importance within contemporary classroom environments. Online learning has many advantages, like flexibility and accessibility, but it also brings up important questions about equality and access.

Let's examine these issues in-depth, using real-world examples to highlight the difficulties and possible fixes.

7.2.1. Advantages of Online Education:

1. **Adaptability and Practicality:**

-   **Example:** To upskill at their own speed, working professionals can sign up for online courses through sites like Coursera or edX.
-   **Explanation:** Because online learning is accessible from anywhere at any time, it is a convenient option for those with different schedules and responsibilities.

1. **Vast Selection of Resources:**

-   **Example:** For instance, having access to e-books, digital libraries, and online seminars.
-   **Justification:** Students' access to a wide range of online learning resources and content improves their knowledge base and overall learning experience.

1. **Personalised Learning:**

- **Example:** For K–12 educations, adaptive learning systems such as DreamBox provide an example.
- **Justification:** Learning experiences can be customized to meet the needs of each individual student using online education systems, which enable individual learning trajectories and rates.

1. **Global Learning Community:**

- **Example:** For instance, collaborative projects and discussion boards on websites like Canvas or Blackboard.
- **Justification:** Peers from various cultural and geographic origins can collaborate and engage with one another because to the global learning community that online education creates.

7.2.2. Accessibility Issues

1. **The Digital Divide**

- **Example:** For instance: Students in remote locations without access to high-speed internet.
- **Explanation:** The difference between people who have access to contemporary information and communication technology and people who do not is known as the "digital divide." This gap may make it more difficult for students in underprivileged areas to engage completely in online learning.

1. **Device Accessibility:**

- **Example:** A household with restricted access to tablets or computers is an example.
- **Justification:** It's possible that a large number of students lack

personal gadgets or must share a single device with family members, which makes it difficult for them to participate in online learning successfully.

1. **Technical Proficiency:**

- **Example:** Students who are older or come from a low-tech background and find it difficult to use online resources.
- **Justification:** In order to engage in online learning efficiently, teachers and students must possess a particular degree of digital literacy. A major obstacle may be the absence of these abilities.

1. **Assistance Services:**

- **Example:** For instance, not being able to get online therapy, tutoring, and other forms of support.
- **Explanation:** Students' success and general learning experience may be impacted by the fact that traditional support services they depend on may not be as readily available online.

7.2.3. Equity-Related Issues:

1. **Social and Economic Divides:**

- **Example:** For instance, low-income students might not be able to purchase modern technology or dependable internet connections.
- **Explanation:** A student's capacity to engage in online learning can be strongly impacted by socioeconomic circumstances. Resolving these discrepancies is necessary to guarantee equitable access.

1. **Accommodations for Disabilities:**

- **Example:** For instance, there are online resources that children with hearing or vision problems cannot completely access.
- **Justification:** Equity requires that all students, including those with impairments, have access to online learning environments. This entails offering captions for films, alternate text for photos, and screen reader compatibility.

1. **Language Barriers:**

- **Example:** English-only content proving difficult for non-native speakers of the language.
- **Justification:** Content on online learning platforms is frequently available exclusively in English, which may be detrimental to non-native speakers. Offering multilingual support can assist in lessening this problem.

1. **Instructional Quality:**

- **Example:** Variability in the level of instructor preparation and the quality of online courses.
- **Justification:** It's critical to provide excellent training in online courses. This entails preserving strict academic standards and educating educators on online teaching techniques.

7.2.4. Solutions and Strategies:

1. **Enhancing Facilities:**

- **Example:** Examples include efforts by the public and

commercial sectors to increase broadband availability in rural areas.

- **Justification:** It's imperative to make infrastructural investments to ensure that every location has dependable internet connection. In the US, initiatives like the FCC's E-Rate program assist schools and libraries in obtaining reasonably priced broadband.

1. **Supplying Devices:**

- **Example:** An illustration would be school districts giving pupils laptops or iPads.
- **Explanation:** By giving students access to the essential hardware, educational institutions and organizations can close the device gap. This problem is being addressed by programs such as Google's classroom Chromebook initiative.

1. **Digital Literacy Training:**

- **Example:** Giving instructors and students workshops on digital skills, for instance.
- **Justification:** Conducting training programs aimed at enhancing digital literacy guarantees that all attendees are able to utilize online learning environments efficiently. Digital literacy classes are a common feature of university curricula.

1. **Ensuring Accessibility:**

- **Example:** Using Universal Design for Learning (UDL) principles in the creation of online courses is one example.
- **Justification:** Ensuring equal learning opportunities requires designing online courses that are accessible to all students, including those with disabilities. This entails offering content

in a variety of formats and utilizing accessible channels.

1. **Support in Multiple Languages:**

- **Example:** Providing course materials in several languages is one example.
- **Justification:** Giving non-native speakers access to materials and assistance in many languages can improve their comprehension and interaction with the material. Language deficits can be filled using classes offered in several languages on platforms like Duolingo.

1. **Assisting Students from Lower Incomes:**

- **Example:** Examples include grants, scholarships, and affordable internet services.
- **Justification:** Students from low-income families may be able to cover the expenses of online education with the aid of financial aid programs. These students may also benefit from partnerships with internet service providers that offer lower pricing.

In summary, there is a lot of potential for improving learning outcomes and increasing access to education with online education. However, it is essential to address fairness and access concerns in order to fully reap its benefits. We can establish a fairer and inclusive online learning environment by assisting low-income students, guaranteeing accessibility, supplying digital literacy training, enhancing infrastructure, and supporting multilingual education. We can make sure that every kid has the chance to thrive in the digital age by putting these efforts into action.

7.3. Challenges and Opportunities in Digital Learning Environments

Digital learning environments, which offer individualized, adaptable, and accessible learning experiences, have completely changed the educational landscape. Nevertheless, in order to fully realize their potential, they also pose a number of hurdles that must be overcome. Let's explore the opportunities and problems in digital learning settings from the perspective of an IT specialist, using concrete examples to support our arguments.

7.3.1. Difficulties in Digital Learning Settings:

1. **The Digital Gap:**

- **Example:** For instance, students in low-income or rural areas might not have access to modern technology or high-speed internet. \
- **Explanation:** The difference between people who have access to technology and the internet and those who do not is known as the "digital divide." Many students may find it difficult to engage in productively in digital learning environments as a result of this difference.

1. **Motivating and Engaging:**

- **Example:** A dearth of engagement and interesting material is causing students to lose interest in online courses.
- **Justification:** Compared to traditional classrooms, online environments might present challenges for maintaining student interest because of distractions, a lack of in-person connection, and the delivery of less compelling content.

1. **Technical Problems:**

- **Example:** During online classes, there are often problems with connectivity, software bugs, and platform outages.
- **Justification:** Technical issues can interfere with learning, leading to annoyance and a waste of important teaching time. These problems may originate from the platform itself as well as from the user.

1. **Content Consistency and Quality:**

- **Example:** Differences in the calibre of courses provided by various platforms or organizations.
- **Justification:** For learning to be effective, high-quality and consistent content must be provided across a variety of platforms and courses. Knowledge gaps may result from inconsistencies.

1. **Evaluation and Academic Honesty:**

- **Example:** For instance, it can be challenging to stop people from cheating on online tests and evaluations.
- **Justification:** It can be difficult to uphold academic integrity in a digital setting. To guarantee accuracy and impartiality, reliable proctoring systems and creative evaluation techniques are needed.

1. **Training and Readiness of Instructors:**

- **Example:** Teachers finding it difficult to adjust to digital teaching resources and techniques.
- **Explanation:** Compared to traditional classroom teaching, effective online teaching calls for various skill sets. It's possible

that a lot of teachers lack the expertise and self-assurance required to successfully teach online courses.

7.3.2. Possibilities in Online Learning Environments

1. Personalised Learning:

- **Example:** For instance, adaptive learning systems such as Knewton and DreamBox.
- **Justification:** By customizing content and pacing according to each student's performance and preferences, digital learning environments can offer individualized learning experiences. Students' comprehension and retention may improve as a result of this customisation.

1. Reaching a Global Audience:

- **Example:** For instance, edX and Coursera are examples of MOOCs (Massive Open Online Courses) systems.
- **Justification:** By enabling educational institutions to reach a worldwide audience, digital learning platforms make it possible for students to receive a top-notch education wherever they may be.

1. Convenience and Flexibility:

- **Example:** One illustration would be asynchronous courses that let learners progress at their own speed.
- **Explanation:** Students can fit their studies around other responsibilities, like employment or family, thanks to the flexibility that online learning gives in terms of time and place.

1. Rich and Diverse Content:

- **Example:** Multimedia components like simulations, interactive tests, and videos can be included as an example.
- **Justification:** A greater range of content kinds are available on digital platforms, which improves learning's comprehensiveness and engagement. Different learning styles can be accommodated by interactive and multimedia content.

1. **Collaborative Learning:**

- **Example:** Group projects utilizing Microsoft Teams and Zoom, as well as online discussion boards.
- **Justification:** Through online group discussions and activities, digital learning environments can help students collaborate and communicate with one another, encouraging peer learning and teamwork.

1. **Expense-effectiveness:**

- **Example:** Less material and physical infrastructure required.
- **Justification:** Both educational institutions and learners may find online instruction to be more economical. It lowers total costs by eliminating the need for travel, printed materials, and physical classrooms.

7.3.3. Addressing Challenges to Maximise on Opportunities

1. **Overcoming the Digital Divide:**

- **Example:** Giving underprivileged students inexpensive internet plans and gadgets is one example.
- **Justification:** In the United States, programs like the FCC's E-Rate program assist schools and libraries in obtaining

reasonably priced broadband. Offering equipment at a discount can also aid in closing the gap.

1. **Increasing Involvement:**

- **Example:** Platforms for gamified learning such as Kahoot! and Duolingo provide one example.
- **Justification:** Real-time feedback, interactive information, and gamification can all help to boost student motivation and engagement. Interactive talks and live virtual sessions also aid in sustaining attention.

1. **Enhancing the Technical Framework:**

- **Example:** Purchasing dependable and expandable online education systems is one example.
- **Justification:** It's critical to have a dependable technical infrastructure with little downtime and user-friendly interfaces. Technical problems can be avoided with routine maintenance and updates.

1. **Providing High-Quality Content:**

- **Example:** Working together to create courses with organizations and knowledgeable teachers.
- **Justification:** Peer review procedures and collaboration with seasoned instructors can support the upkeep of high standards for the content of online courses.

1. **Creative Techniques for Assessment:**

- **Example:** Using open-book exams with project-based assessments is one example.

- **Justification:** Using a variety of evaluation techniques outside of the exam will help gauge students' comprehension more accurately and cut down on cheating. Academic integrity can also be preserved with the use of technologies like AI-based proctoring.

1. **Support and Training for Teachers:**

- **Example:** Programs for professional development that emphasize digital teaching techniques are one example.
- **Explanation:** Instructors can become more used to online teaching techniques by receiving thorough training and continuous assistance. Online materials, webinars, and workshops can help them advance professionally.

In summary, many opportunities exist to improve education through personalized learning, flexibility, and accessibility in digital learning settings. To take full use of these potential, however, obstacles including the digital divide, engagement, technological problems, high-quality content, integrity of assessments, and instructor preparedness must be overcome. Educational institutions may establish equitable and productive digital learning environments that cater to the requirements of every student by putting focused solutions and tactics into practice.

Chapter 8: Health and Well-Being in the Digital Age

8.1. Telemedicine and Remote Health Monitoring

By utilizing technology to increase the availability, effectiveness, and quality of medical care, telemedicine and remote health monitoring have become revolutionary forces in the healthcare industry. Let's dive into the specifics of these developments as IT professionals, examining their advantages, difficulties, and real-world applications.

8.1.1. Telemedicine:

8.1.1.1. Definition of Telemedicine: Telemedicine is the practice of providing patients with clinical information and healthcare services remotely by means of telecommunication technology. This covers remote diagnosis, video consultations, and even prescription drug writing without the necessity for a face-to-face meeting.

8.1.1.2. Telemedicine's Advantages

8.1.1.2.1. Enhanced Healthcare Access:

- **Example:** For instance, patients in underprivileged or rural locations can consult with experts in large cities.
- **Explanation:** Patients can obtain medical care without having to travel great distances thanks to telemedicine, which eliminates geographical limitations. People who live in rural areas with limited access to healthcare services would especially benefit from this.

8.1.1.2.2. Practicality and Effectiveness:

- **Example:** An illustration would be online consultations through services like Doctor on Demand and Teladoc.

- **Justification:** By allowing patients to consult with medical professionals from the comfort of their homes, telemedicine provides convenience. As a result, there is less need for travel and waiting, which improves healthcare delivery efficiency overall.

8.1.1.2.3. Continuity of Treatment:

- **Example:** Scheduling follow-up visits and managing chronic illnesses.
- **Explanation:** To explain, telemedicine makes it easier to monitor patients continuously and provide follow-up care, which is essential for managing chronic illnesses like diabetes or hypertension. Frequent virtual check-ins support prompt intervention and plan modifications.

8.1.1.2.4. Savings on costs:

- **Example:** A decrease in the requirement for hospital admissions and ER visits.
- **Explanation:** Patients and healthcare systems can save a great deal of money by using telemedicine to provide prompt medical advice and care in the event of difficulties that could otherwise result in expensive ER visits or hospital stays.

8.1.2. The Challenges with Telemedicine:
8.1.2.1. Technological Obstacles:

- **Example:** Certain places have restricted access to high-speed internet.
- **Justification:** Reliable internet access and the right equipment are necessary for effective telemedicine, but not all

patients will have access to these, especially in rural or low-income locations.

8.1.2.2. Security and Privacy Issues:

- **Example:** As an illustration, make sure that laws like HIPAA are followed.
- **Justification:** Platforms for telemedicine need to guarantee patient data security and confidentiality. Maintaining patient privacy requires adherence to laws like the Health Insurance Portability and Accountability Act (HIPAA).

8.1.2.3. Integrating with Traditional Healthcare Systems:

- **Example:** Managing telemedicine in conjunction with in-person consultations and medical records is one example.
- **Justification:** It can be difficult to integrate telemedicine with the current medical systems and electronic health records (EHR). In order to guarantee continuity and comprehensiveness of care, seamless coordination is required.

8.1.3. Remote Health Monitoring:

8.1.3.1. Definition: This is the process of gathering patient health data in real time using digital devices and sensors, then sending it to healthcare personnel for review and supervision. In particular, post-acute care and the management of chronic diseases benefit greatly from this technique.

8.1.3.2. The Advantages of Remote Health Surveillance

8.1.3.2.1. Real-Time Gathering of Data:

- **Example:** An example would be wearable technology that tracks exercise levels and heart rate, such as the Fitbit or Apple Watch.
- **Justification:** By continuously gathering health data, these gadgets offer real-time information about a patient's state. This makes it possible to identify irregularities quickly and to seek medical attention when needed.

8.1.3.2.2. Better Management of Chronic Illnesses:

- **Example:** For example, glucose monitors can help manage diabetes.
- **Justification:** By giving patients and medical professionals access to real-time glucose readings, devices like continuous glucose monitors (CGMs) enable better diabetes management through prompt pharmacological and lifestyle modifications.

8.1.3.2.3. Enhanced Involvement of Patients:

- **Example:** An example would be smartphone apps that monitor prescription adherence and report symptoms.
- **Justification:** Patient participation in health management is facilitated by the use of remote monitoring systems. Treatment plan adherence can be enhanced by apps that prompt users to report symptoms or take their meds.

8.1.3.2.4. Decrease in Readmissions to Hospitals:

- **Example:** Patients recovering from surgery are monitored remotely.
- **Justification:** Through remote patient monitoring following surgery, medical professionals can detect possible issues early

on and take preventative action, which lowers the risk of readmissions.

8.1.3.3. Difficulties with Telemedicine Monitoring
8.1.3.3.1. Overloading with Data:

- **Example:** Organizing massive amounts of data from several patients is one example.
- **Justification:** Healthcare practitioners may become overwhelmed by the constant stream of data from remote monitoring devices. To choose and order pertinent data, effective data management and analytics technologies are required.

8.1.3.3.2. Device Accuracy and Reliability:

- **Example:** For instance, making sure wearable health monitoring are accurate.
- **Justification:** Accuracy and dependability of remote monitoring tools are essential to providing quality care. To guarantee that they deliver precise and useful data, devices need to undergo extensive testing and validation.

8.1.3.3.3. Patient Education and Compliance:

- **Example:** Ensuring appropriate device use by patients.
- **Justification:** In order to use remote monitoring equipment properly, patients must receive the appropriate training. Improper use or noncompliance might result in incomplete data and inefficient monitoring.

8.1.3.3.4. Regulatory and Compensation Concerns:

- **Example:** For instance, navigating insurance reimbursement for services provided by remote monitoring.
- **Justification:** The laws governing remote health monitoring are still being developed. It can be difficult to make sure these services adhere to legal requirements and are insured.

8.1.4. Examples of Remote Health Monitoring and Telemedicine in Practice
8.1.4.1. Teladoc Health

- **Justification:** Teladoc Health is a top telemedicine firm that provides online consultations with physicians, specialists, and mental health providers. It serves as an example of how telemedicine may offer easily accessible and convenient medical treatments.

8.1.4.2. Livongo:

- **Justification:** Livongo offers remote health monitoring services for long-term medical issues like high blood pressure and diabetes. Their platform offers individualized health insights and coaching by fusing data analytics with smart device integration.

8.1.4.3. Babylon Health:

- **Justification:** To explain, Babylon Health integrates AI-powered health assessments with telemedicine. Their app improves accessibility and preventive care by providing AI-powered symptom checkers and video consultations with physicians.

8.1.4.4. Philips HealthSuite:

- **Justification:** The cloud-based platform Philips HealthSuite combines information from multiple health monitoring devices. It gives medical professionals the ability to remotely monitor patients and provide useful information to enhance patient outcomes.

In summary, healthcare is changing because telemedicine and remote health monitoring make it more convenient, effective, and individualized. Although there are many advantages to these technologies, there are also issues that must be resolved if their full potential is to be reached. Enhancing telemedicine and remote health monitoring can lead to better patient care and outcomes by removing technology obstacles, protecting privacy and security, integrating with conventional healthcare systems, and resolving regulatory concerns.

8.2. Mental Health and Social Media

Given the ubiquitous nature of social media platforms in contemporary life, the relationship between mental health and these platforms is an important field of study for an IT professional. In addition to its many advantages—such as communication and information exchange—social media poses serious threats to one's mental health. We go into more detail on each of these below, giving instances to highlight the significance.

8.2.1. Beneficial Social Media Impacts on Mental Health:

8.2.1.1. Support Networks:

- **Example:** An example would be Facebook or Reddit online support groups for people with particular mental health concerns.
- **Justification:** Social media sites give users a place to interact with people who have gone through comparable struggles and experiences. These support groups can be especially helpful for people who are feeling alone since they can provide emotional support, guidance, and a sense of community.

8.2.1.2. Access to Mental Health Resources:

- **Example:** For instance, the National Alliance on Mental Illness (NAMI) and other mental health groups use Instagram and Twitter to disseminate resources and information.
- **Justification:** Mental health groups may swiftly and extensively distribute important information by using social media. By giving users access to materials on coping mechanisms, warning signs of mental illness, and where to get treatment, the platform raises awareness and offers

instructional material.

8.2.1.3. **Advocacy and Awareness:**

- **Example:** Examples include social media campaigns to combat the stigma associated with mental health, such as #BellLetsTalk on Twitter.
- **Justification:** Social media can help raise awareness of mental health issues by connecting with a wide audience and encouraging constructive dialogue about mental health. These initiatives can lessen stigma and motivate people to get care.

8.2.1.4. **Educational and Healing Content:**

- **Example:** For instance, licensed therapists' Instagram and YouTube pages that provide advice on coping mechanisms and mental wellbeing.
- **Justification:** Practitioners can provide instructional films, mindfulness practices, and therapeutic information on social media platforms for users to view whenever it's convenient for them. Practical techniques for managing stress, anxiety, and other mental health concerns can be found in this content.

8.2.2. **Social Media's Harmful Effects on Mental Health**
8.2.2.1. **Cyberstalking and Mistreatment:**

- **Example:** For instance, people are the subject of trolls and cyberbullies on social media sites like Instagram and Twitter.
- **Explanation:** Because of the anonymity and accessibility of social media, victims of cyberbullying may experience anxiety, despair, or even thoughts of suicide. Harassment can manifest itself in a variety of ways, such as planned attacks, doxxing, and offensive remarks.

8.2.2.2. Comparison and Problems with Self-Esteem:

- **Example:** One example might be Instagram influencers that showcase extremely manicured and perfected lifestyles.
- **Justification:** Low self-esteem and feelings of inadequacy can result from a lifetime of exposure to unrealistic pictures and lifestyles. Users run the risk of worsening conditions like depression and body dysmorphia by comparing themselves to these unattainable ideals.

8.2.2.3. Time Management and Addiction:

- **Example:** An example might be someone who spends too much time on Facebook or TikTok and neglects their obligations in real life.
- **Reason:** Because social media has elements that are meant to keep people interested for a long time, it might be addicting. This may disrupt regular tasks, work output, and sleep cycles.

8.2.2.4. Anxiety and Overload of Information:

- **Example:** For instance, you are constantly exposed to news and information on international problems on Twitter.
- **Justification:** An abundance of knowledge, especially bad news, can cause information overload and increased worry. This behaviour, which is sometimes called "doomscrolling," can make people feel more stressed and powerless.

8.2.3. Reducing the Effect: Techniques and Illustrations
8.2.3.1. Education for Digital Literacy:

- **Example:** One example is the implementation of digital literacy programs in schools to instruct pupils on responsible usage of social media.

- **Justification:** Adequate user education regarding the dangers of social media, privacy issues, and responsible usage practices can help to lessen the bad effects. Programs can concentrate on controlling screen time, identifying cyberbullying, and critically analysing internet content.

8.2.3.2. Software and Apps for Mental Health:

- **Example:** For instance, apps that teach mindfulness and meditation techniques, such as Headspace and Calm.
- **Justification:** By offering resources for stress relief, mental wellbeing, and relaxation, mental health applications can be used in conjunction with social media use. These applications support users in maintaining their mental health by providing guided meditations, breathing techniques, and mood monitoring tools.

8.2.3.3. Modifications to Algorithms and Content Control:

- **Example:** To ease comparison anxiety, Instagram users can hide their likes.
- **Justification:** In order to counteract cyberbullying and harassment, social media businesses can adjust their algorithms to favour positive content and enforce more stringent content control policies. These platforms have the potential to lessen negative effects by fostering a more secure and encouraging online community.

8.2.3.4. Expert Assistance and Virtual Counselling:

- **Example:** Online counselling sessions are provided by

BetterHelp and Talkspace.

- **Explanation:** Users can have remote counselling sessions with professional therapists using online therapy platforms. These services facilitate easier access to mental health support, particularly for individuals who are unable to attend in-person meetings.

8.2.4. Examples and Case Studies
8.2.4.1. Facebook's Resources for Preventing Suicide:

- **Explanation:** Facebook has integrated artificial intelligence (AI) capabilities to identify posts that may indicate suicidal ideation and offer users relevant resources and support. Additionally, friends have the option to flag questionable content, which prompts Facebook to provide information about crisis help.

8.2.4.2. Instagram's #HereForYou Campaign:

- **Justification:** As part of its #HereForYou initiative, Instagram invites users to share their experiences with mental health and ask for community help. The program seeks to dispel the stigma attached to mental health problems and promote a supportive atmosphere.

8.2.4.3. The Wellness Guides on TikTok:

- **Justification:** TikTok has incorporated wellness guidelines and suggestions to motivate people to pause and consider how they use social media. These manuals offer advice on controlling screen use and preserving a positive social media presence.

In summary, social media use and mental health have a complicated relationship that includes both positive and negative aspects. Social media can be a great source of community, support, and information, but it also comes with a number of serious hazards, such the possibility of addiction, comparison-induced anxiety, and cyberbullying. We can optimize the positive effects while reducing the negative effects of social media on mental health by putting measures like digital literacy education, mental health app promotion, and improved content moderation into practice.

8.3. Ethical Considerations in Health-related Technologies

Artificial intelligence (AI) in diagnostics, wearable technology, telemedicine platforms, electronic health records (EHRs), and other developments are all included in the category of health-related technologies. Although these technologies have many advantages, there are also serious ethical questions they bring up. In order to guarantee that technological innovations, have a good impact on healthcare, it is imperative that IT professionals comprehend and tackle these ethical concerns.

8.3.1. Confidentiality and Privacy:

8.3.1.1. Electronic Health Records (EHRs) are one example.

- **Problem:** A lot of sensitive patient data, such as diagnoses, treatment plans, and medical histories, are stored in electronic health records (EHRs). Data breaches or unauthorized access can result in serious privacy violations.
- **Justification:** It's critical to protect patient information's confidentiality. Unauthorized access to sensitive health data can result in identity theft, stigmatization, and prejudice.
- **Solution:** Put in place frequent security audits, access controls, and strong encryption techniques. For example, the Health Insurance Portability and Accountability Act (HIPAA) in the United States establishes strict guidelines for the security of medical records.

8.3.2. Informed Consent:

8.3.2.1. Genetic Testing and Personal Genomics as an Example:

- **Problem:** Businesses such as 23andMe sell genetic testing services that tell people about their hereditary susceptibilities to different diseases. Users might not really comprehend the consequences of this knowledge, though.
- **Justification:** Patients must be aware of the possible results, dangers, and restrictions associated with a medical test or treatment in order to give their informed consent. This is especially difficult when it comes to complicated technology like genetic testing, where the results can have far-reaching and unclear effects.
- **Solution:** Give explicit, thorough explanations of the test's possible results and ramifications. To make sure everyone understands, use interactive consent procedures like decision aids or films.

8.3.3. Data Integrity and Accuracy
8.3.3.1. Wearable Medical Technology – as an Example:

- **Problem:** Health measurements such as heart rate, physical activity, and other data are collected by devices such as fitness trackers and smartwatches (e.g., Fitbit, Apple Watch). Inaccurate data can result in erroneous health assessments and actions.
- **Justification:** Having accurate and trustworthy health data is essential to make wise health decisions. Inaccurate information has the potential to mislead medical professionals and patients, resulting in ineffective interventions or treatments.
- **Solution:** To guarantee accuracy, validate and update the algorithms these devices utilize on a regular basis. Urge consumers to double-check wearable data with expert medical advice.

8.3.4. Access and Equity
8.3.4.1. For Instance, Telemedicine:

- **Problem:** Many people now have better access to remote healthcare services thanks to telemedicine platforms like Teladoc and Doctor on Demand. But there's a chance that those without dependable internet access or low digital skills will fall behind.
- **Justification:** Technology has the potential to exacerbate health disparities by creating a larger divide between those who have access to contemporary healthcare services and those who do not.
- **Solution:** Create initiatives to raise digital literacy levels and offer reasonably priced internet access. To target underprivileged populations, provide telemedicine services through neighbourhood health clinics or community centres.

8.3.5. Fairness and Bias:
8.3.5.1. For Instance, AI in Diagnostics:

- **Problem:** Because AI algorithms are educated on data from various sources, they may display biases when employed in diagnostic applications, like IBM Watson Health. Lack of diversity in the training data could cause the AI to function differently in diverse groups.
- **Justification:** Disparities in diagnosis and treatment resulting from bias in health-related AI can disproportionately impact specific demographic groups.
- **Solution:** Make sure the training data for AI is representative of the whole population and diversified. Keep an eye out for bias in AI systems, audit them frequently, and modify the algorithms as necessary.

8.3.6. Independence and Management:
8.3.6.1. For Instance, Remote Patient Monitoring:

- **Problem:** Real-time data collection and transmission to healthcare providers is facilitated by remote monitoring equipment, including continuous glucose monitors used for diabetes management. Although advantageous, patients may experience a loss of autonomy over their health data and a sense of being watched all the time.
- **Justification:** Patients ought to be in charge of their health information, with the power to determine who has access to it and how it is used.

  Solution: Put in place clear data policies and give patients authority over their information, including the ability to choose whether or not to share it. Inform patients about the advantages of remote monitoring and how their data will be used.

8.3.7. Professional and Patient-Provider Relationship:
8.3.7.1. Virtual Health Assistants as an Example:

- **Problem:** Chatbots that offer medical advice are examples of virtual health assistants that can occasionally take the place of or enhance the work of real healthcare professionals.
- **Justification:** The relationship between a patient and a provider is crucial for trust and may be impacted by the depersonalization of healthcare. When communicating with automated systems, patients could feel less supported and understood.
- **Solution:** Use virtual assistants to enhance in-person communication rather than to replace it. Make certain that patients may receive emotional support and more advanced medical care from licensed healthcare professionals.

8.3.8. Accountability and Transparency:
8.3.8.1. Clinical Decision Support Systems, for instance:

- **Problem:** Healthcare professionals use clinical decision support systems (CDSS) to help them make decisions about diagnosis and treatment. However, it may be challenging to comprehend and accept these systems' recommendations if their decision-making procedures are opaque.
- **Justification**: Trust and accountability in the use of health-related technology depend on their operational transparency. Patients and providers alike should be aware of the rationale behind the suggestions made by these systems.
- **Solution:** Create AI systems and models that are understandable and intuitive. Give thorough details about the decision-making process.

In summary, technologies connected to health have the power to completely transform the industry, increasing access to services and boosting results. The patient-provider relationship, privacy, informed permission, data accuracy, equity, bias, autonomy, and openness are just a few of the important ethical issues that these technologies also bring up. Ensuring that health-related technologies benefit everyone equally and responsibly requires addressing these ethical challenges through strong policies, education, and technology protections. By doing this, we can respect and safeguard patients' rights and well-being while utilizing technology to improve healthcare.

Chapter 9: Politics and Governance in the Digital Age

145

9.1. Social Media and Political Engagement

Social media has completely altered the terrain of political participation by revolutionizing the means of communication and mobilization for individuals, organizations, and governments. It's critical for IT professionals to comprehend the ways in which social media affects political participation as well as the larger ramifications for democracy and society. We explore these points in more detail and provide examples below.

9.1.1. Social Media's Beneficial Effects On Political Engagement

9.1.1.1. Improved Access to Information:

- **Example:** As an illustration, consider Facebook and Twitter as news distribution channels.
- **Justification:** Users of social media platforms have access to a variety of political news and information from many sources. Citizens will find it simpler to remain informed about political events, policies, and debates as a result of this democratization of information. Politicians, journalists, and activists may keep the public informed in real time.

9.1.1.2. Encouraging Political Activation:

- **Example:** An illustration of this would be the Arab Spring and social media.
- **Justification:** Social media has shown itself to be an effective instrument for planning and energizing political movements. Social media sites like Facebook and Twitter were used during the Arab Spring to organize demonstrations, disseminate

news about governmental initiatives, and mobilize support for democratic reforms. These platforms made quick organizing and communication possible, which was essential to the movements' success.

9.1.1.3. Increasing Involvement in Politics:

- **Example:** Online petitions and crowdsourcing for political campaigns are two examples.
- **Justification:** By giving people the means to participate in politics, social media lowers the obstacles to political engagement. People can support causes and push for policy changes by creating online petitions on sites like Change.org. Political candidates and activists can gather money for their campaigns through crowdfunding websites like GoFundMe, which expands involvement beyond conventional fundraising techniques.

9.1.1.4. Facilitating Straightforward Communication:

- **Example:** As an illustration, consider how politicians interact with voters directly on social media.
- **Justification:** Social media platforms give politicians a direct line of communication with the public, avoiding the gatekeepers of traditional media. Politicians may become more approachable and receptive to the issues of their voters as a result of this open dialogue. For instance, former US President Barack Obama communicated his policy views and engaged voters on Twitter and Facebook in a successful manner.

9.1.1.5. Promoting Political Conversation:

- **Example:** Examples of hashtags are #MeToo and #BlackLivesMatter.
- **Justification:** Public dialogue on significant political and social issues is made possible by social media platforms. Global discussions on gender equality and racial injustice have been aided by hashtags like #MeToo and #BlackLivesMatter, respectively. Social media has been a tool utilized by these movements to create communities, spread awareness, and accelerate social change.

9.1.2. Negative Social Media's Effects On Political Participation:

9.1.2.1. Dissemination of Misinformation and Disinformation:

- **Example:** A case in point is the dissemination of false information amid the 2016 American presidential contest.
- **Justification:** Misinformation and disinformation can travel quickly through social media platforms, misleading people and undermining democratic processes. Fake news reports proliferated on social media during the 2016 U.S. presidential election, swaying public opinion and possibly influencing the result of the vote.

9.1.2.2. Echo Chambers and Polarization:

- **Example:** For instance, algorithms on Facebook and YouTube are generating filter bubbles.
- **Justification:** Social media algorithms frequently give users' pre-existing opinions and preferences first priority, producing "echo chambers" where people are only exposed to information that supports their opinions. As a result, consumers are less likely to come across opposing viewpoints,

which can exacerbate political polarization and split public conversation.

9.1.2.3. **Cyberstalking and Mistreatment:**

- **Example:** For instance, harassing female activists and politicians online.
- **Justification:** Social media sites can be unfriendly places, especially for women and other underrepresented groups. Cyberbullying and harassment are commonplace for female politicians and activists, which can deter political engagement and muzzle critical voices. Prominent female politicians, such as Alexandria Ocasio-Cortez, have documented prolonged instances of cyberbullying.

9.1.2.4. **Manipulation and Operations of Influence:**

- **Example:** An instance of this would be Russian meddling in the 2016 US elections via social media.
- **Justification:** Influencers, both local and foreign, can use social media to sway public opinion and carry out influence operations. In an effort to sow discord and erode trust in democratic institutions, the Russian Internet Research Agency (IRA) utilized social media platforms to disseminate hate speech and meddle in the 2016 US elections.

9.1.2.5. **Limited Attention Duration and Surface-Level Engagement:**

- **Example:** An illustration would be the prevalence of short content, such as memes and tweets.
- **Justification:** Social media's design promotes the consumption of brief, readily absorbed content, which may

result in a cursory understanding of complicated political matters. Short films, memes, and tweets frequently oversimplify complex subjects, shallowing the depth of public conversation and comprehension.

9.1.3. Methods for Overcoming the Obstacles:
9.1.3.1. Development of Media Literacy:

- **Example:** One example would be educational initiatives in schools that promote digital literacy and critical thinking.
- **Justification**: Enhancing media literacy can lessen the impact of false and misleading information by assisting users in critically analysing the content they come across on social media. To enable people to traverse the digital information ecosystem, educational programs that teach critical thinking and digital literacy skills are crucial.

9.1.3.2. Regulation and Transparency in Algorithms:

- **Example:** As an illustration, consider Facebook's initiatives to increase the transparency of its news feed algorithms.
- **Justification:** Social media firms should take action to prevent echo chambers from forming and be more open about how their algorithms rank information. Policies that support algorithmic accountability and transparency can help guarantee that these platforms act in the public interest.

9.1.3.3. Enhancing The Moderation of Content:

- **Example:** For instance, Twitter's guidelines prohibiting harassment and hate speech.
- **Justification:** Strict content moderation guidelines are required to stop the spread of damaging content including

cyberbullying and harassment. Although Twitter and other platforms have put policies in place to deal with harassment and hate speech, users still need to be protected, which calls for ongoing enforcement and development.

9.1.3.4. Encouraging Diverse Views:

- **Example:** Programs like cross-political discussions that provide exposure to a range of perspectives.
- **Justification:** Promoting exposure to a variety of viewpoints can aid in balancing out polarization. Public conversations that are more inclusive and balanced can be fostered by programs that support cross-political conversations and content that presents various points of view.

9.1.3.5. Countering Influence Operations:

- **Example:** An instance of collaboration may be the identification and mitigation of foreign influence by social media businesses and government authorities.
- **Justification:** To detect and thwart influence activities, cooperation between governments, civil society organizations, and social media firms is essential. The goal of initiatives like Facebook's collaboration with the Digital Forensic Research Lab at the Atlantic Council is to identify and reduce foreign intervention in elections.

In summary, political participation has been profoundly altered by social media, which presents both opportunities and difficulties. It has made political mobilization easier, information access more democratic, and citizen-politician dialogue more direct. On the other hand, technology has additionally aided in the dissemination of false information, divisiveness in politics, and cyberbullying. A multimodal strategy is needed to address these issues, one that includes boosting media literacy, advocating for algorithm openness, fortifying content control, supporting a diversity of viewpoints, and opposing influence operations. We may use social media to encourage political discourse and democratic participation by carefully managing these challenges.

9.2. E-Government and Digital Democracy

Digital democracy and e-government are innovative strategies that use information technology to boost citizen participation, streamline government operations, and create more inclusive and effective democratic processes. It is essential for an IT specialist to have a thorough understanding of these ideas, including their applications, advantages, and difficulties. Here, we examine these facets using real-world examples to highlight the significance and promise of digital democracy and e-government.

9.2.1. E-Government:

9.2.1.1. **Definition and Implementation:** The term *"e-government"* describes how government organizations use digital technology to interact with the public, deliver services, and enhance internal processes. Electronic data management, digital communication channels, and online service delivery are the main constituents.

9.2.1.2. **E-Government Initiative Examples Include**:

1. **Portals for Online Services:**

- **Example:** In the UK, Gov.uk is one example.
- **Justification:** The Gov.uk portal combines a number of government services onto a single, easily navigable webpage. Online access to services including tax payments, passport renewals, and benefit applications increases convenience and effectiveness for citizens.

1. **Digital Identity Systems:**

- **Example:** Consider Estonia's e-Residency initiative.
- **Explanation:** Through its e-Residency program, Estonia provides both residents and non-residents with a digital identity. By enabling remote business start-up, electronic document signing, and access to Estonian e-services, this digital ID promotes the growth of the digital economy.

1. **E-Voting (Electronic Voting) Systems:**

- **Example:** Switzerland's e-voting trials are one example.
- **Justification:** To enable residents to cast ballots online for elections and referendums, a few Swiss cantons have experimented with electronic voting. The goal of this approach is to make voting more accessible in order to raise voter participation.

1. **Mobile Government Apps:**

- **Example:** The Unified Mobile Application for New-age Governance (UMANG) app from India is one example.
- **Justification:** The UMANG app allows residents to access services including healthcare, education, and municipal services from their cellphones by combining several government functions into a single mobile application.

9.2.2. Digital Democracies:

9.2.2.1. Definition and Implementation: Using digital technologies and platforms to improve democratic processes—such as citizen participation in decision-making, openness, and accountability—is known as *"digital democracy."* It includes online voting, consultation, and involvement.

9.2.2.2. Initiatives for Digital Democracy Examples:

1. **Budgeting with Participation**:

- **Example:** For instance, the participatory budgeting platform of the city of Paris.
- **Explanation:** Via an online portal, citizens of Paris are able to suggest and cast votes on the budget allocations for community initiatives. Through this program, voters will have direct control over local government spending.

1. **Online Consultation Tools:**

- **Example:** The "Your Voice in Europe" platform from the European Union is one example.
- **Justification:** EU people can comment on proposed laws, policies, and projects using this website. It seeks to guarantee that people's voices are heard and to include them in the policymaking process.

1. **Open Data Initiatives:**

- **Example:** Data.gov, for instance, is the US equivalent.
- **Justification:** The federal government makes its datasets available to the public through Data.gov. Government data can be used by people, researchers, and developers for a variety of objectives, such as innovation, research, and holding the government responsible, thanks to this transparency program.

1. **Public Engagement via Digital:**

- **Example:** The Icelandic constitutional change process, for instance.

- **Justification:** Iceland involved its people in the process of writing a new constitution by using a crowdsourcing method. Social media and internet platforms allow citizens to share thoughts and opinions, promoting inclusive and participatory governance.

9.2.3. Benefits of E-Government and Digital Democracy:

1. **Enhanced Effectiveness:**

- **Explanation:** Digital services expedite service delivery, cut down on paperwork, and streamline government processes. Online tax filing methods, for example, can drastically minimize processing times and errors.

1. **Improved Availability:**

- **Explanation:** Services are available around-the-clock, no matter where you are, thanks to e-government platforms. For people living in rural or isolated areas who might not have easy access to actual government offices, this is very helpful.

1. **Savings on costs:**

- **Explanation:** By eliminating the need for physical infrastructure and manual processing, digitizing services can result in significant cost savings for governments. For instance, switching to e-procurement technologies can improve procurement efficiency and save administrative expenses.

1. **Enhanced Openness and Responsibility:**

- **Explanation:** By making information easily accessible to the public, open data programs and digital interaction platforms promote government openness. This promotes government accountability and trust.

1. **Increased Involvement of Citizens:**

- **Explanation:** By enabling citizens to participate in policymaking, consultations, and voting from the comfort of their homes, digital democracy technologies promote more inclusive involvement. Governance as a result may become more responsive and representative.

9.2.4. Challenges and Considerations:

1. **The Digital Divide:**

- **Explanation:** There are differences in access to digital technology depending on factors including education, social class, and location. This digital divide has the potential to widen the gap between rich and poor, preventing disadvantaged populations from fully gaining from e-government and digital democracy programs.
- **Solution:** To close the digital divide, governments should fund digital infrastructure, offer reasonably priced internet access, and support initiatives that increase digital literacy.

1. **Privacy and Security Issues:**

- **Explanation:** Because e-government systems manage private information, they are vulnerable to hackers. It is essential to ensuring this data's security and privacy.
- **Solution:** Put in place strong cybersecurity safeguards

including multi-factor authentication, encryption, and recurring security audits. To secure personal information, follow data protection laws and best practices.

1. **Opposition to Change:**

- **Explanation:** Due to unfamiliarity or fear of losing their jobs, both citizens and government workers may oppose the shift to digital systems.
- **Solution:** To facilitate the transition, offer assistance and training to both employees and residents. To promote adoption, emphasize the advantages of digital technologies and aggressively resolve any reservations.

1. **Ensuring Inclusivity:**

- **Explanation:** All citizens, including those with disabilities or low levels of computer competence, should be able to use digital platforms.
Resolution: While creating e-government services, adhere to accessibility guidelines and universal design principles. Provide people who are unable to use one way to access another way.

1. **Preserving Democratic Integrity:**

- **Explanation:** In order to preserve the integrity of democratic processes, electronic voting and online participation technologies need to be safe and dependable. Voter fraud, hacking, and technological issues can all raise questions that erode public trust in digital democracy.
- **Solution:** The answer is to create and thoroughly test safe electronic voting systems. To make sure that digital

democratic practices are reliable and honest, use open, auditable procedures.

In summary, the management of public services by governments has significantly improved thanks to e-government and digital democracy. Governments can improve citizen participation, accessibility, efficiency, and transparency by utilizing digital technologies. But in order to fully reap these benefits, issues like the digital gap, privacy and security concerns, change-aversion, inclusion, and the integrity of democratic processes must be addressed. We can use technology to make governance systems that are more inclusive, responsive, and efficient by carefully managing these obstacles.

9.4. Challenges of Regulating Information and Communication Technologies

Information and communication technologies (ICT) are subject to a wide range of complex regulations because of the internet's worldwide reach, the speed at which technology is developing, and the variety of stakeholder interests. It is imperative for an IT professional to have a thorough understanding of these issues and how they affect organizations, users, and legislators. We examine the main issues below with pertinent examples.

9.4.1. Rapid Technological Advancement:

- **The Challenge:** The rate of technological advancement surpasses the capacity of regulatory structures to maintain pace. Regulatory gaps occur when new technologies develop more quickly than the laws and rules intended to control them.
- **Example:** *Blockchain Technology and Cryptocurrencies*: While Bitcoin and other cryptocurrencies quickly gained traction, many nations found it difficult to create legal frameworks that addressed problems like money laundering, tax evasion, and fraud. Because blockchain technology is decentralized and unchangeable, it complicates regulatory monitoring. This is one of the issues associated with blockchain technology, which powers cryptocurrencies.
- **Implications:** To foresee and address developing innovations, policymakers need to collaborate closely with technologists and embrace flexible, adaptive regulatory approaches.

9.4.2. The Global Nature of ICT:

- **Challenge:** ICT operates internationally, making it challenging for a single nation to adequately govern. Conflicts and discrepancies may result from disparate national laws and regulations.
- **Example:** *Data Privacy*: Businesses operating in the EU or managing the data of EU people are subject to stringent data protection regulations set forth in the General Data Protection Regulation (GDPR). Multinational corporations face compliance issues due to disparate or laxer data privacy rules in various nations.
- **Implications:** To manage the global nature of ICT, international cooperation and harmonization of rules are required. Organizations must navigate diverse regulatory frameworks to achieve compliance across jurisdictions.

9.4.3. Handling the Challenge of Innovation and Regulation:

- **Challenge:** Rules are important to safeguard consumers and preserve fair markets, but they can also hinder innovation and economic expansion if they are too strict. Achieving the ideal balance is essential.
- **Example:** *Ride-sharing Services:* As they upended established taxi services, businesses like Uber and Lyft encountered legal issues. Regulations were put in place to protect consumers and promote fair competition, but if they were too onerous, they might impede the development and advantages of these novel services.
- **Implications:** Regulators need to work with consumers and industry participants to create fair regulations that safeguard interests without unreasonably impeding innovation.

9.4.4. The Challenge of Safeguarding Consumer Privacy:

- **Challenge:** It is getting harder and harder to protect consumer privacy in the age of big data and ubiquitous surveillance. ICT businesses gather enormous volumes of personal data, which raises questions about how this information is handled and safeguarded.
- **Example:** *Facebook-Cambridge Analytica Scandal*: It was discovered in 2018 that millions of Facebook users' personal information had been collected by Cambridge Analytica without their knowledge or permission and was being used for political advertising. This case brought to light serious shortcomings in the laws and enforcement surrounding data protection.
- **Implications:** To secure consumer data, stronger privacy laws—like the GDPR—and effective enforcement strategies are required. Businesses must get users' express consent and have transparent data processing procedures.

9.4.5. The Challenge of Cybercrime and Cybersecurity:

- **Challenge:** Cyberattacks and cybercrime are becoming more common as our reliance on ICT increases. Ensuring strong cybersecurity defences while upholding civil rights and privacy is a difficult regulatory task.
- **Example:** *Ransomware Attacks:* Well-known ransomware attacks, like the 2017 WannaCry attack, impacted enterprises all around the world, including hospitals and other vital infrastructure. The aforementioned occurrences underscored the necessity of all-encompassing cybersecurity rules and global collaboration in the fight against cybercrime.
- **Implications:** In order to combat the worldwide nature of cyber threats, governments must create and implement strict cybersecurity regulations as well as encourage international cooperation. Public-private collaborations can also improve

the resilience of cybersecurity.

9.4.6. The Challenge of Free Speech and Content Moderation:

- **Challenge:** It's a fine line to regulate internet content to protect free speech rights while preventing hate speech, disinformation, and other damaging content.
- **Example:** *Social Media Regulation:* There is a lot of pressure on websites like Facebook, YouTube, and Twitter to control what is posted. However, the standards for eliminating content might be debatable and differ among legal jurisdictions, sparking discussions about free speech and censorship.
- **Implications:** Content moderation requires oversight procedures and clear, unambiguous norms. Governments, platforms, and civil society organizations working together can create well-rounded strategies that protect free speech while minimizing harm.

9.4.7. The Challenge of Digital Divide and Access Inequality:

- **Challenge:** It is imperative to guarantee fair access to ICT and tackle the issue of the digital divide. Inequalities in social and economic status can be made worse by differences in technology access.
- **Example:** *Rural Broadband service:* Unreliable internet service in rural and underserved areas limits opportunities for healthcare, work, and education in many nations. In the US, initiatives like the FCC's Connect America Fund attempt to close this disparity, while difficulties still exist.
- **Implications:** To guarantee that ICT is widely available and

reasonably priced, policymakers must make infrastructure investments and develop inclusive policies. Moreover, public-private collaborations can aid in closing the digital gap.

9.4.8. Ethical AI and Automation Use:

- **Challenge:** The application of automation and AI brings up ethical issues related to transparency in decision-making, employment displacement, and bias.
- **Example:** *AI in Hiring:* It has been discovered that hiring algorithms, like those used by Amazon, are biased against particular groups of people, which results in unfair hiring procedures. Fairness, accountability, and transparency in AI systems are important regulatory issues.
- **Implications:** Provisions for ethical use, accountability, and transparency should be included in AI and automation regulations and standards. It takes ongoing observation and assessment to reduce prejudices and other moral dilemmas.

In summary, the regulation of information and communication technologies entails managing the ethical application of artificial intelligence (AI), addressing the digital divide, safeguarding consumer privacy, maintaining cybersecurity, regulating content, and navigating the rapidly advancing technological landscape. For regulations to be effective, various stakeholders—including governments and business—must collaborate and adapt.

Regulators can establish settings that support innovation while defending the rights and interests of all stakeholders by being aware of and responding to these problems.

Chapter 10: Politics and Governance in the Digital Age

10.1. Data Privacy: Balancing Individual Rights and Corporate Interests

In today's digital world, when businesses gather, process, and store enormous amounts of personal data, data privacy is a crucial problem. It is a complicated and multidimensional task to strike a balance between people's right to privacy and businesses' interests in using data for innovation and financial gain.

Here, we examine the main problems, obstacles, and strategies for striking this balance, using real-world examples to highlight the ideas.

10.1.1. **Recognizing the Privacy of Data:** The right of individuals to manage the collection, use, and sharing of their personal data is known as *data privacy*. This includes safeguarding personal information against abuse, disclosure, and illegal access. Consent, openness, data minimization, and security are important facets of privacy.

10.1.2. **The Significance of Data Privacy:**

- *Individual Rights*: Preserving personal data is essential to preserving one's liberties, dignity, and independence. It stops data misuse that can result in discrimination, identity theft, and other negative outcomes.
- *Trust:* Maintaining data privacy promotes trust between people and institutions. Users are more likely to use digital services when they believe their data is handled ethically.
- *Adherence to Regulations*: Respecting data privacy laws, such the CCPA in California or the GDPR in the EU, is crucial to staying out of trouble with the law and upholding one's good name.

10.1.3. **Business Interests in Data Utilization**:
Businesses gather and examine personal information for a number of reasons:

- *Personalization:* Personalized services, recommendations, and content that improve user experiences.
- *Marketing:* Increasing the effectiveness of marketing by using targeted advertising to reach particular groups.
- *Innovation* is the process of creating new goods and services using insights from customer data.
- *Operational Efficiency*: Using data analytics to improve decision-making processes and streamline operations.

10.1.4. **Difficulties in Judging Interests and Rights**:

1. **Informed Consent:**

- **Example:** For instance, a lot of consumers provide their consent to data collecting without reading or comprehending privacy regulations. This raises questions about how informed consent actually is.
- **Approach:** Make privacy policies more easily comprehensible by using plain language. Provide granular consent systems that allow users to select which particular data they feel comfortable sharing.

1. **Minimization of Data:**

- **Example:** For instance, Facebook and other social media sites gather a lot of data—often more than is required for the services they offer. This might cause overreaching.
- **Approach:** Use data reduction guidelines, gathering only the information required to fulfil the goal. Consistent audits can

guarantee adherence to these guidelines.

1. **Transparency:**

- **Example:** For instance, the Cambridge Analytica incident exposed the lack of awareness among Facebook users over the use of their personal information for political advertising and profiling.
- **Approach:** Increase openness by outlining the procedures for gathering, using, and sharing data. Transparency can be increased using interactive tools that inform consumers of the data collected and its intended purpose.

1. **Security:**

- **Example:** Well-known data breaches, like the Equifax incident, have revealed millions of individuals' private information, exposing them to financial loss and identity theft.
- **Approach:** Put strong security measures in place, such as encryption, frequent security audits, and timely breach reporting. Strong cybersecurity procedures guard user information against breaches and illegal access.

1. **Data Portability:**

- **Example:** For instance, customers might wish to move between service providers without jeopardizing their data. This is especially true for social networking and cloud storage providers.
- **Approach:** Enable users to export their data in a common format with simple-to-use tools, hence facilitating data portability. Competition and user control over personal data

are encouraged by this.

10.1.5. **Regulatory Structures and Their Impacts:**
10.1.5.1. **General Data Protection Regulation (GDPR):**

- **Example:** For instance, the GDPR enables users to seek data deletion (the right to be forgotten) and mandates that businesses obtain explicit agreement before collecting personal data. It also requires businesses to notify users of data breaches within 72 hours.
- **Impact:** GDPR has raised the bar for data privacy and influenced international data security procedures. Businesses' operations and data strategy will be impacted by the investment they must make in compliance procedures.

10.1.5.2. **The California Consumer Privacy Act (CCPA):**

- **Example:** Californians, for instance, have the right to know what personal data is collected, to request its deletion, and to refuse to have their data sold. In addition, noncompliance is subject to sanctions.
- **Impact:** The CCPA has forced businesses to re-evaluate and modify their data practices in order to meet its standards, which has resulted in more extensive modifications to the way personal data is managed.

10.1.6. **Technological Approaches to Strengthen Security:**
10.1.6.1. **Privacy-Enhancing Technologies (PETs):**

- **Example:** As an illustration, firms can obtain insights without disclosing specific data points by using differential privacy approaches, which introduce noise into data sets. Apple gathers usage data via differential privacy, which protects user privacy.

10.1.6.2. Encryption:

- **Example:** For instance, end-to-end encryption in messaging apps such as WhatsApp guarantees that the messages are only readable by the persons involved, preventing third parties from intercepting the data.

10.1.6.3. Using Anonyms and Pseudonyms:

- **Example:** An illustration of this would be the anonymization of healthcare data to enable study and examination without disclosing patient identities. Pseudonymization lowers the possibility of data misuse by substituting pseudonyms for identifying information.

10.1.7. Business Ethics and Responsibility:
10.1.7.1. Frameworks for Data Ethics:

- **Example:** For instance, Microsoft's AI ethics guidelines cover values including accountability, inclusivity, openness, safety, privacy, and fairness. These rules aid in guaranteeing moral data practices.

10.1.7.2. Data Stewardship for Companies:

- **Example:** As an illustration, Google's Project Strobe, which was launched in response to the Google+ data breach, involved a careful examination of data privacy regulations and third-party access to user data. This resulted in stricter controls and increased transparency.

10.1.8. **Education and Empowerment of Users:**

10.1.8.1. **Educating Users:**

- **Example:** Examples of initiatives that support education and awareness of data privacy rights and best practices are Data Privacy Day and others. Users that are educated are better able to make judgments with their data.

10.1.8.2. **Empowering Tools:**

- **Example:** Platforms such as Facebook and Google give consumers the ability to adjust permissions, evaluate collected data, and modify their choices for data sharing.

In summary, it's a complex and continuous task to strike a balance between business interests and individual rights regarding data privacy. It calls for a blend of user empowerment, technology solutions, moral corporate conduct, and regulatory compliance. Corporations can establish credibility and guarantee appropriate data utilization while utilizing data for innovation and expansion by implementing all-encompassing approaches that give precedence to transparency, security, and user control. A balanced ecosystem that respects both business interests and individual privacy can be created by combining effective legislation with proactive corporate accountability and educated user interaction.

10.2. Government Surveillance and Civil Liberties

The term "government surveillance" describes how government organizations keep an eye on people, groups, or data, frequently for the sake of law enforcement or national security. Although monitoring can improve public safety and reduce crime, it also poses serious issues with respect to basic rights such as the right to privacy, the freedom of speech, and the ability to protest. Understanding the intricate interactions between civil liberties and government monitoring, as well as the ramifications and instances of these tactics, is crucial for IT professionals.

10.2.1. Government Surveillance Types:

There are several ways that the government can monitor its citizens:

1. **Electronic Surveillance:** keeping an eye on communications via text, email, phone, and the internet.

- **Example:** For instance, the National Security Agency (NSA) in the US has participated in numerous electronic monitoring initiatives, like PRISM, which gathers information from significant internet firms like Google, Facebook, and Apple.

1. **Physical Surveillance:** Tracking people's movements and physical areas using cameras, drones, and other technology.

- **Example:** As an illustration, consider the widespread usage of CCTV cameras for public space surveillance in the United Kingdom, especially in urban areas.

1. **Data Surveillance**: Gathering and examining enormous datasets, commonly known as "big data," in order to spot trends and behaviours.

- **Example:** Consider China's Social Credit System, which gathers information from a range of sources—such as social, financial, and legal records—in order to evaluate the conduct of its citizens and issue ratings that may have an impact on their ability to access certain services.

10.2.2. Advantages of Government Surveillance:

1. **National Defence:**

- **Example:** As an illustration, post-9/11 surveillance programs in the US were designed to stop terrorist strikes by keeping an eye on communications for possible threats.

1. **Law enforcement and Crime Prevention:**

- **Example:** For instance, police agencies utilize data analysis software and surveillance cameras to track down offenders and keep an eye on high-crime areas.

1. **Security for the Public:**

- **Example:** An illustration would be the use of monitoring at major public gatherings like the Olympics to keep an eye out for any security risks and control crowds.

1. **Impact on Civil Liberties:**

1. **Privacy:**

- **Concern:** Constant monitoring and unapproved data collecting might result from surveillance, which violates people's right to privacy.
- **Example:** For instance, the disclosures made public by Edward Snowden revealed how the National Security Agency's mass data gathering initiatives secretly recorded millions of Americans' conversations.

1. **Expression Rights:**

- **Concern:** People may self-censor and refrain from voicing opposing or controversial opinions if they are aware that they are being observed.
- **Example:** For instance, people in nations like China who have strict internet control and monitoring policies would refrain from talking about politically touchy subjects online.

1. **Right to Assemble:**

- **Concern:** People may be discouraged from taking part in demonstrations or voicing their political opinions if public meetings and protests are being watched.
- **Example:** Concerns were expressed regarding the potential chilling impact on activists' desire to engage when Black Lives Matter protests in the US were being monitored.

1. **The Presumption of Innocence and Due Process:**

- **Concern:** By profiling and targeting people based on patterns and algorithms, surveillance may avoid following the normal legal procedures.
- **Example:** As an illustration, predictive policing algorithms that use data analysis to find probable suspects or crime

hotspots may perpetuate prejudices and unfairly single out particular communities.

10.2.3. A Look at Legal and Ethical Issues:

1. Legal Structures and Supervision:

- **Example:** For instance, the United States' Foreign Intelligence Surveillance Act (FISA) lays out guidelines for monitoring foreign intelligence targets. Nonetheless, questions about accountability and openness have been brought up by the FISA courts' covert character.

1. Ethical Technology Use:

- **Concern:** When implementing technology like AI and facial recognition in surveillance, ethical considerations including bias, accuracy, and misuse potential need to be taken into account.
- **Example:** For instance, law enforcement has come under fire for using facial recognition technology because of concerns that it could mistakenly identify people, especially those who are people of colour.

10.2.4. Harmonizing Civil Liberties with Surveillance:

1. Openness and Responsibility:

- **Approach:** Through independent monitoring organizations, governments should guarantee accountability and be transparent about their surveillance operations.
- **Example:** As an illustration, consider the appointment of privacy commissioners or ombudsmen to supervise

monitoring operations and respond to public complaints.

1. Need and Proportionality:

- **Approach:** The extent of surveillance activities should be commensurate with the threat and required to accomplish a justifiable goal.
- **Example:** Rather than gathering large amounts of data in bulk, restrict surveillance to particular, well-defined targets.

1. Protections & Safeguards:

- **Approach:** Putting in place legal protections, like requiring warrants for surveillance operations and offering protection to those who reveal illegal surveillance.
- **Example:** For instance, the European Court of Human Rights' decisions in cases involving state monitoring underscore the importance of stringent legal protections.

1. Public Discussion and Participation:

- **Method:** Holding public conversations regarding surveillance techniques and how they affect civil freedoms.
- **Example:** For instance, holding public hearings and consultations on proposed surveillance regulations would let people express their concerns and influence policy.

10.2.5. Technological Approaches to Strengthen Privacy:

1. Encryption:

- **Example:** As an illustration, end-to-end encryption in messaging apps such as WhatsApp and Signal guarantees that the conversations are only readable by the parties involved, shielding them from prying eyes and even government monitoring.

1. **The Process of Anonymization**:

- **Example:** As an illustration, users can anonymize their internet activity using tools like Tor and VPNs (Virtual Private Networks), which makes it more challenging for monitoring organizations to monitor their online activity.

1. **Technologies that Enhance Privacy (PETs)**:

- **Example:** For instance, businesses like Apple employ differential privacy strategies to gather aggregate data without jeopardizing individual privacy.

In summary, while necessary for maintaining public safety and national security, government surveillance seriously compromises civil freedoms, including the right to privacy, the freedom of speech, and the ability to protest. A complex strategy that takes legal protections, ethical considerations, accountability, and openness into account is needed to strike a balance between these objectives. Societies may negotiate the complexity of monitoring and maintain core civil rights while addressing security concerns by putting in place strong oversight mechanisms and having public debates. In an era of ubiquitous surveillance, technological solutions such as encryption and privacy-enhancing technology are also essential for protecting individual privacy.

10.3. The Ethics of Surveillance Technologies

Modern society is becoming more and more dependent on surveillance technologies, such as facial recognition, CCTV cameras, and sophisticated data analytics. These technologies present serious ethical issues in addition to their many advantages in terms of security, crime prevention, and operational effectiveness. It is crucial for an IT professional to comprehend these moral issues and investigate how they affect both people and society at large.

10.3.1. Privacy Invasion:

- **Concern:** Without their awareness or consent, surveillance technologies have the potential to invade people's privacy by gathering and analysing data about them.
- **Example:** *Smart Home Appliances*: Appliances such as Google Home and Amazon Echo are always listening for voice requests. These gadgets have occasionally unintentionally recorded private talks, which has raised worries about unintentional spying.
- **Ethical Implications:** One of the most basic human rights is privacy. Unchecked, ongoing surveillance has the potential to undermine individual liberty and foster a culture of fear and self-censorship.

10.3.2. Transparency and Consent:

- **Concern:** A lot of surveillance techniques are opaque, and people frequently don't give their informed consent for data collection and use.
- **Example:** *Social Media Monitoring*: Websites such as

Facebook and Instagram gather a tonne of information about the activities of their users. Most of the time, users are ignorant about the scope of data collection and its use to customized advertising.

- **Social Consequences:** A fundamental component of moral data gathering is informed consent. Consumers ought to be fully informed about the types of data being gathered, how they will be used, and who will have access to it.

10.3.3. Data Security and Misuse:

- **Concern:** Surveillance systems can gather data that is susceptible to breaches and misuse, which could result in serious consequences.
- **Example:** *Equifax Data Breach*: A significant credit reporting agency, Equifax, experienced a data breach in 2017 that resulted in the exposure of 147 million people's personal data. This had addresses, birth dates, and Social Security numbers.
- **Social Consequences:** It is morally required of organizations to secure the data they gather. Inadequate data security can result in identity theft, financial loss, and other grave repercussions for individuals.

10.3.4. Bias and Discrimination:

- **Concern:** Discriminatory results may arise from surveillance technologies, especially those that use AI and machine learning. These technologies have the potential to reinforce and even increase biases.
- **Example:** *Facial Recognition Technology*: Research has indicated that women, persons of colour, and other marginalized groups may experience greater mistake rates while using facial recognition software. For instance, a 2019

National Institute of Standards and Technology (NIST) study discovered considerable differences in accuracy among various demographic groups.

- **Social Consequences**: In order to utilize surveillance technologies ethically, biases must be acknowledged and mitigated. Failing to do so may result in vulnerable communities being unfairly targeted and subjected to prejudice.

10.3.5. Freedom of Expression and Assembly:

- **Concern:** People's willingness to join in public gatherings and freely express themselves may be inhibited by the existence of surveillance.
- **Example:** *Monitoring of Protests*: Law enforcement organizations employed facial recognition software, drones, and other surveillance technologies to keep an eye on demonstrators during the 2020 Black Lives Matter demonstrations in the United States. Concerns regarding the freedom of expression and assembly were raised by this.
- **Social Consequences:** It is improper to utilize surveillance to stifle legitimate opposition or prevent people from exercising their democratic rights. These essential liberties must be respected and upheld by ethical surveillance tactics.

10.3.6. Accountability and Oversight:

- **Concern:** When surveillance technologies are not properly regulated, those in positions of authority may abuse them, which would erode public confidence.
- **Example:** Law enforcement uses stingray devices to capture mobile phone communications, but these tools have drawn criticism for their potential for abuse and lack of openness.

Their use has eschewed judicial oversight in certain instances.

- **Social Consequences:** Ensuring that surveillance technologies are utilized responsibly and ethically requires strong accountability measures. This entails open policies, frequent audits, and independent body supervision.

10.3.7. Restrictions on Use and Minimization of Data Fear:

- **Concern:** Mission creep occurs when information gathered for one reason is used for another without the permission of the original users.
- **Example**: *Smart City Projects*: Information gathered by smart city projects—such traffic cameras or environmental sensors—may be utilized for unrelated objectives like commercial profiling or law enforcement.
- **Social Consequences:** The ethical application of surveillance technologies necessitates explicit restrictions on the uses of data. Data should not be collected for unapproved uses and should only be used for specified, legal purposes.

10.3.8. Global Disparities and Digital Colonialism:

- **Concern:** The use of surveillance technologies by wealthy countries or firms to spy on weaker ones can both reflect and exacerbate global inequality.
- **Example:** *Export of Surveillance Technologies*: Authoritarian regimes can employ the surveillance technologies that industrialized countries export to their citizens in order to monitor and repress them.
- **Social Consequences:** Cross-border ethical considerations apply. Businesses and governments should think about how their technologies might affect human rights and refrain from

supporting repressive actions around the world.

In summary, *the ethics of surveillance technologies entail striking a balance between the preservation of human rights and civil liberties and the advantages of efficiency and security.* Privacy invasion, permission and transparency, data security, bias and discrimination, freedom of assembly and expression, accountability, purpose limitation, and worldwide disparities are some of the major ethical issues. A diverse strategy is needed to address these issues, one that includes strong legislative frameworks, moral standards, technology protections, and proactive public involvement. By doing this, we may ensure that surveillance technologies contribute to a just and equitable society by maximizing their potential benefits while reducing any potential drawbacks.

Chapter 11: Cybercrime and Cybersecurity

11.1. Understanding Cybercrime: Types and Motivations

Illegal activities carried out via computers, networks, or the internet are referred to as *cybercrime*. These offenses include everything from fraud and theft to more complex assaults like cyberespionage and hacking. It is essential to comprehend the many forms of cybercrime and the reasons behind them in order to create cybersecurity measures that work.

11.1.1. Cybercrime Types

11.1.1.1. Hacking:

- **Synopsis:** illegal access to data, networks, or computer systems.
- **As an illustration**: *Yahoo Data Breach (2013–2014):* Three billion accounts were breached, allowing hackers to obtain personal data such names, email addresses, and security questions.
- *Sony PlayStation Network Attack (2011)*: Credit card details and other personal information were taken by hackers from 77 million accounts.

11.1.1.2. Phishing:

- **Synopsis:** fraudulent emails or websites that deceive people into divulging personal information, like bank account information or login credentials.
- **As an illustration:** *Google Docs Phishing Scam (2017):* The perpetrators tricked victims into allowing access to their email accounts by sending phony invitations to Google Docs.
- *Phishing emails purporting to be from PayPal:* Frequently

occurring frauds in which victims receive spoof emails asking for account verification in order to obtain login credentials.

11.1.1.3. **Ransomware:**

- **Synopsis:** malware that encrypts a target's files and demands a ransom to unlock the key.
- **As an illustration**: *The WannaCry attack of 2017* disrupted services in government offices, businesses, and hospitals, affecting over 230,000 computers across 150 countries. Bitcoin was sought as ransom by the attackers.
- *Colonial Pipeline Attack (2021):* Fuel shortages and a $4.4 million ransom payment resulted from a ransomware attack on a significant US pipeline operator.

11.1.1.4. **Identity Theft:**

- **Synopsis:** the theft of personal data for fraudulent purposes, such as establishing credit cards or bank accounts in the victim's name.
- **As an illustration:** In *the 2017 Equifax data breach*, hackers took 147 million people's personal information, including their Social Security numbers. This resulted in multiple identity theft cases.
- *Target Data Breach (2013):* 40 million customers' credit and debit card details as well as 70 million people's personal information were taken by cybercriminals.

11.1.1.5. **Distributed Denial of Service (DDoS):**

- **Synopsis:** flooding a network or website with so much traffic that it becomes unusable for users.
- **As an illustration**: *2016 saw the Dyn Cyberattack, a*

significant DDoS attack against DNS provider Dyn that caused major website outages, including Reddit, Twitter, and Netflix.

- The biggest DDoS attack to date, *the GitHub DDoS Attack (2018)* temporarily brought down the software development platform with traffic reaching a peak of 1.35 Tbps.

11.1.1.6. Cyber Espionage:

- **Synopsis:** spying on people, businesses, or governments in order to obtain private information.
- **As an illustration:** *Operation Aurora (2009):* a cyberespionage effort purportedly carried out by Chinese hackers to steal intellectual property that targeted Google and other significant corporations.
- *2020 SolarWinds Hack*: Russian state-sponsored hackers are suspected of carrying out a cyberattack on the IT management company SolarWinds, which resulted in security vulnerabilities in a number of US government departments and commercial businesses.

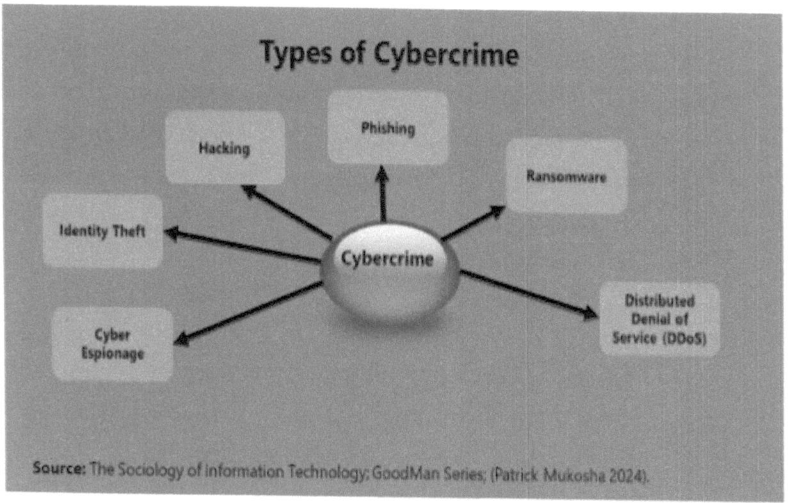

Figure 1: Types of Cybercrime

11.1.2. The Reasons for Cybercrime

11.1.2.1. Monetary Gain:

- **Synopsis:** Profit is the main driving force behind the actions of many cybercriminals. This may entail outright stealing, deception, or blackmail.
- **As an illustration:** *Business Email Compromise (BEC) Scams*: By breaching executive email accounts, cybercriminals deceive businesses into sending substantial amounts of money.
- *Cryptojacking* is the illegal use of another person's computer to mine cryptocurrencies and make money off of the processing power without that person's permission.

11.1.2.2. Hacktivism: Political or Ideological Motivations

- **Synopsis:** attacks that are committed in protest, to further a political cause, or to draw attention to a social concern.

- **As an illustration**: *Anonymous* is a hacktivist group that has targeted corporate, religious, and governmental websites repeatedly in an effort to advance free speech and other causes.
- *Operation Payback (2010):* A string of denial-of-service assaults launched by Anonymous against groups that oppose WikiLeaks.

11.1.2.3. Activities Sponsored by the State:

- **Synopsis:** cyber operations carried out by a nation-state or on its behalf in order to get intelligence, interfere with infrastructure, or affect international relations.
- **As an illustration:** *(2010) Stuxnet:* An advanced malware that was allegedly developed by Israel and the United States to target industrial control systems and undermine Iran's nuclear program.
- *Russian Meddling in the US Election of 2016:* cyberattacks and email leaks from the Democratic National Committee are examples of actions intended to sway the results of the US presidential election.

11.1.2.4. Personal Motivations or Vengeance

- **Synopsis:** personal grievance-driven attacks that frequently target former employees or other people.
- **As an illustration**: *Disgruntled Employee Attacks*: In an effort to exact revenge, former employees who feel mistreated may steal information or compromise networks.
- *Celebrity hacks*: Hackers driven by a personal grudge or a desire for recognition frequently target the personal information of celebrities.

11.1.2.5. Corporate Espionage:

- **Synopsis:** Businesses that steal intellectual property or trade secrets in order to obtain a competitive advantage.
- **As an illustration**: In the *2017 lawsuit Google v. Uber, Waymo*, a division of Google, claimed that Uber had engaged in cyberespionage through which it had stolen technology secrets related to self-driving cars.
- *(2011) DuPont Trade Secrets Theft*: Workers were discovered offering Chinese businesses confidential knowledge regarding DuPont's production method for titanium dioxide.

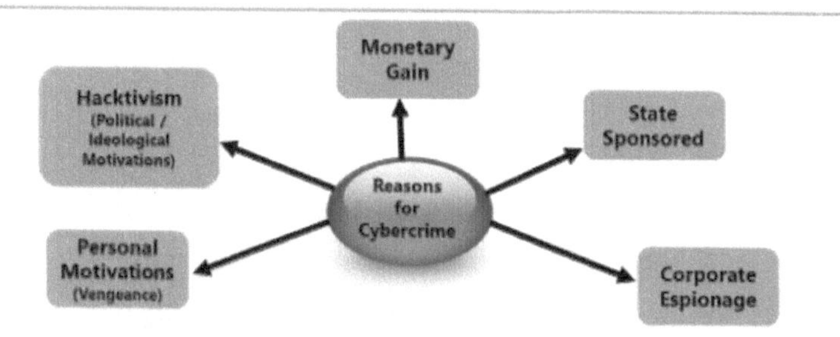

Source: The Sociology of Information Technology; GoodMan Series; (Patrick Mukosha 2024).

Figure 2: Reasons for Cybercrime

In summary, a thorough understanding of the many kinds of cyberattacks and the varied reasons behind them is necessary to comprehend cybercrime. The motivations behind cybercriminals are as diverse as their techniques, ranging from personal grudges and state-sponsored espionage to monetary gain and political activism. People and organizations can better plan for and protect against cybercrime by understanding these risks and the fundamental reasons behind them. This will ensure increased security and resilience in the digital era.

11.2. Strategies for Cybersecurity and Data Protection

To secure sensitive information and maintain business continuity in today's digital environment, people, corporations, and governments must prioritize cybersecurity and data protection. It is critical for an IT professional to comprehend and put into practice efficient methods to reduce cyberthreats. Here's a thorough breakdown of several tactics, along with clear illustrations when applicable.

11.2.1. Risk Assessment and Management:

- **Description:** recognizing, assessing, and ranking the threats to the information assets of a company.
- **Techniques:**
    - *Frequent Risk Assessments:* Regularly assessing potential weak points and dangers.
    - *Risk Mitigation Plans:* Creating and carrying out plans to mitigate hazards that have been recognized is known as risk mitigation.
- **As an illustration:** *Banking Sector*: Banks adopt measures to secure online transactions and client data, and they undertake risk assessments to guard against financial crime.

11.2.2. Network Security:

- **Description:** safeguarding data availability, confidentiality, and integrity while it's being transferred over or accessible via networks.
- **Techniques:** *Firewalls:* Filtering traffic according to security rules, they serve as barriers separating trustworthy and untrusted networks.

- *Intrusion Detection and Prevention Systems (IDPS):* keeping an eye on network activity for unusual activity and taking appropriate action in case of an intrusion.
- **As an illustration:** *Corporate Network*: To safeguard their worldwide network architecture against cyber threats, major organizations such as Google employ sophisticated network security measures including firewalls and intrusion detection systems (IDPS).

11.2.3. Endpoint Security:

- **Description:** safeguarding individual network-connected devices, including PCs, tablets, and smartphones.
- **Techniques:**
    - *Software for Antivirus and Anti-Malware*: identifying and eliminating harmful software from endpoints.
    - *Endpoint Detection and Response (EDR):* delivering responsiveness and ongoing monitoring.
- **As an illustration:** *Bring Your Own Device (BYOD) Policy*: Employers who adopt BYOD policies use EDR solutions to protect employee-owned devices that access company information.

11.2.4. Data Encryption:

- **Description:** converting data into an unintelligible format during transmission and storage to prevent unwanted access.
- **Techniques:**
    - *Encryption Protocols:* Encrypting data using standards such as AES (Advanced Encryption Standard).
    - *Transport Layer Security (TLS) and Secure Sockets Layer (SSL):* data transmission over the internet

using encryption.

- **As an illustration:** *Online stores:* During transactions, SSL/ TLS is used by online retailers such as Amazon to encrypt client data, including payment information.

11.2.5. Access Control and Authentication:

- **Description:** making ensure that only people with permission can access particular data or systems.
- **Techniques:**
  - *Multi-Factor Authentication (MFA):* Demanding several verification methods (password, fingerprint, or one-time password) in order to gain access.
  - *Role-Based Access Control (RBAC):* Giving users permissions according to their responsibilities inside the company.
- **As an illustration:** *Online Banking:* Banks employ multi-factor authentication (MFA) to safeguard client accounts, requiring a password and a code texted to the user's phone in order to log in.

11.2.6. Security Awareness and Training:

- **Description:** teaching staff members and users about cybersecurity recommended practices and threats.
- **Techniques:**
  - *Frequent Training Programs:* Holding seminars and training sessions on handling sensitive data and spotting phishing attempts.
  - *Simulated Attacks:* Phishing attacks can be simulated in order to assess and raise staff knowledge.
- **As an illustration:** *Healthcare Sector:* To protect patient data, hospitals regularly train their employees to identify and report

phishing emails.

11.2.7. **Incident Response and Management:**

- **Description:** creating and putting into place procedures for locating, stopping, and recovering from cybersecurity events.
- **Techniques:**
    - *Incidence Response Plans:* Plans for responding to different kinds of security issues that are documented.
    - *Forensic Analysis:* Investigating incidents to determine their effects and stop them from happening again is known as forensic analysis.
- **As an illustration:** *2017 Equifax Breach Response*: Following a significant data breach, Equifax put in place a comprehensive incident response plan that included informing impacted customers and conducting forensic investigations.

11.2.8. **Frequent Patch Management and Software Updates**

- **Description:** updating software to avoid vulnerabilities that are known to exist.
- **Techniques:**
    - *Automated Updates:* Enabling operating systems and apps to receive updates automatically.
    - *Patch Management Systems:* The process of routinely applying updates to address security flaws.
- **As an illustration:** *Windows OS:* To fix bugs and shield users from possible attacks, Microsoft periodically publishes security updates for Windows.

11.2.9. Data Restore and Backup

- **Description:** making sure that in the event of loss or corruption, data may be restored.
- **Techniques:**
    - *Frequent Backups*: Making regular backups of important information.
    - *Disaster Recovery Plans*: Creating strategies to recover data and resume operations following a cyberattack is known as disaster recovery planning.
- **As an illustration**: *Attacks Using ransomware*: Companies affected by ransomware, such as Colonial Pipeline, depend on backups to get their data back without having to pay the ransom.

11.2.10. Zero Trust Architecture:

- **Description:** a security paradigm that, regardless of whether a person or device is inside or outside the network perimeter, necessitates rigorous verification before granting access to resources.
- **Techniques:**
    - *Constant Monitoring*: Tracking and verifying access requests all the time.
    - *Micro-Segmentation*: Reorganizing the network to manage resource access by breaking it up into smaller sections.
- **As an illustration:** *Google's BeyondCorp*: To protect its systems, Google deployed the Zero Trust security paradigm BeyondCorp.

11.2.11. Requirements for Compliance and Regulations:

- **Description:** obeying the laws and rules pertaining to cybersecurity and data protection.
- **Techniques:**
    - *GDPR Compliance:* Putting the General Data Protection Regulation into practice to safeguard personal information within the European Union.
    - *HIPAA compliance*: Ensuring that healthcare institutions adhere to the Health Insurance Portability and Accountability Act's requirements for patient data security is known as HIPAA compliance.
- **As an illustration:** *Financial Institutions:* To safeguard the financial information of their clients, banks and other financial institutions abide by laws such as the Gramm-Leach-Bliley Act (GLBA).

In summary, a multi-layered strategy that tackles different facets of security, including as risk management, network protection, user education, and incident response, is necessary for effective cybersecurity and data protection. Organizations can improve the security of their information assets by putting these techniques into practice and being aware of the particular threats and vulnerabilities that they are intended to combat.

11.3. Societal Implications of Cybersecurity Threats

Threats to cybersecurity have a significant impact on many aspects of society, including public trust, economic stability, individual privacy, and national security. It is essential for an IT specialist to comprehend these effects and how they affect different facets of society. This is a thorough discussion, backed up by clear examples, of how cybersecurity dangers affect society.

11.3.1. Effect on Privacy and Individual Rights

- **Description:** Cybersecurity risks have the potential to breach individual rights and privacy by allowing unauthorized access to personal data.
- **As an illustration:** *The 2018 Facebook-Cambridge Analytica controversy*: Millions of Facebook users' personal information was taken without their permission and used for political advertising. This privacy violation brought attention to how easily personal information can be misused on social media sites and sparked worries about how it can be used to influence politics.
- **Implications:**
    - loss of faith in social media and internet services.
    - People are becoming more fearful and anxious about the misuse of their personal information.
    - demands more stringent laws and enforcement on data privacy.

11.3.2. Financial Repercussions

- **Description:** Businesses, people, and governments may suffer large financial losses as a result of cybersecurity risks.

- **As an illustration:** *The 2017 NotPetya Cyberattack*: This ransomware attack, which started out targeting Ukraine, moved throughout the world and is estimated to have cost $10 billion in damages. Large corporations suffering major operational interruptions and financial losses were Maersk and FedEx.
- **Implications:**
    - higher expenses for companies as a result of the requirement for improved cybersecurity protections.
    - financial losses as a result of fraud, data breaches, and company interruptions.
    - economic instability in the impacted industries or areas.

11.3.3. Dangers to the Nation's Security:

- **Description:** Threats to cybersecurity have the ability to jeopardize national security and vital infrastructure, which could interrupt vital services.
- **As an illustration:** *(2010) Stuxnet Worm:* An advanced cyberattack tool intended to take down Iran's nuclear installations and stop the nation's uranium enrichment process. This attack served as an example of how strategic military goals could be met without the need for conventional combat by using cyber tools.
- **Implications:**
    - vulnerability of vital infrastructure, including transportation networks, water supplies, and electricity grids.
    - An increase in state-sponsored attacks and cyberwarfare.
    - governments making larger investments in

cybersecurity to safeguard national interests.

11.3.4. Interruptions to Government Services

- **Description:** Cyberattacks have the potential to interfere with public services, impacting residents' daily life.
- **As an illustration:** The attack, known as the Colonial Pipeline Ransomware Attack (2021), caused the temporary closure of one of the biggest fuel pipelines in the United States, resulting in fuel shortages and price increases throughout the Eastern Seaboard. This incident made clear how vulnerable vital infrastructure is to online attacks.
- **Implications:**
  - disruptions to vital services like energy, transportation, and healthcare.
  - Economic disruption and public annoyance resulting from service interruptions.
  - Put pressure on government agencies to strengthen their cybersecurity safeguards.

11.3.5. Effect on Confidence and Trust in the Public

- **Description:** Frequent cyberattacks have the potential to destroy public confidence in organizations, companies, and innovations.
- **As an illustration:** *2017 Equifax Data Breach*: 147 million people's personal information, including credit card numbers and Social Security numbers, was made public. The security hacks exposed weaknesses in Equifax's data protection procedures and seriously eroded consumer confidence in the company.
- **Implications:**
  - reduced faith in governmental organizations,

financial institutions, and IT firms.

- ○ a rise in mistrust and resistance to utilizing new internet services and technologies.
- ○ Call for increased accountability and openness from companies that handle sensitive data.

11.3.6. Impact on Society and Psychology

- **Description:** Threats to cybersecurity can have a psychological effect on people, making them feel stressed, anxious, and vulnerable.
- **As an illustration:** *Identity Theft:* When dealing with money loss, ruined credit, and the protracted process of regaining their identity, victims of identity theft frequently endure high levels of stress and worry.
- **Implications:**
    - ○ Issues with mental health connected to cybersecurity.
    - ○ heightened public knowledge of and apprehension about cyber risks.
    - ○ Resources and support networks are required to assist victims of cybercrime.

11.3.7. Influence on Political Process

- **Description:** Disinformation operations and cyberattacks have the power to sway public opinion and political processes like elections.
- **As an illustration:** *Russian meddling in the US presidential election of 2016:* The goal of cyber operations, including as the DNC hack and the dissemination of false information on social media, was to sway the results of the election and erode public trust in the democratic process.
- **Implications:**

- destruction of democratic structures and procedures.
- an increase in voter polarization and mistrust.
- actions taken to protect election systems and counter misinformation.

11.3.8. Challenges in Education and the Workplace

- **Description:** The growing frequency of cyberattacks demands more attention be paid to workforce development and cybersecurity education.
- **As an illustration:** *Growing Need for Cybersecurity specialists*: Organizations are finding it difficult to fill roles that require protection from cyber-attacks due to a lack of qualified cybersecurity specialists.
- **Implications:**
    - Improved cybersecurity training and education initiatives are required.
    - creation of regulations to draw and keep talent in cybersecurity.
    - spending on ongoing professional development to stay ahead of changing risks.

In summary, Cybersecurity risks have wide-ranging, complex effects on society that include the economy, privacy, public services, trust, mental health, political stability, and education. A comprehensive strategy including strong cybersecurity measures, public awareness campaigns, legal frameworks, and international collaboration is needed to address these ramifications. Through comprehension and mitigation of cyber dangers, we can strive towards a society that is more robust and safe.

Chapter 12: Globalisation and Cultural Identity

201

12.1. Cultural Homogenization vs. Cultural Diversity in the Digital Age

Cultural homogeneity and cultural diversity are two diametrically opposed phenomena that have resulted from the digital age's revolutionary impact on how civilizations interact and change. Comprehending these dynamics and their consequences is essential for an IT specialist to effectively navigate the digital terrain.

12.1.1. Cultural Homogenization:

- **Description:** The process of local cultures becoming more alike is known as "cultural homogenization," and it frequently results in the global culture taking precedence over regional customs and identities.
- **Cultural Homogenization's Motivators:**
    - *Global Media and Entertainment:* Similar cultural standards and values are adopted as a result of the extensive distribution of movies, music, and television series from dominating cultures (mostly Western, notably American).
    - *Social Media Platforms:* Local languages and customs are frequently neglected in favour of international communication on sites like Facebook, Instagram, and Twitter.
    - *Global consumer brands*: Businesses that standardize their products globally, such as McDonald's, Starbucks, and Nike, have an impact on regional tastes and ways of life.
- **As an illustration:**
    - *Hollywood Influence*: Western ideals, ways of life, and storylines are promoted by Hollywood films, which

are watched all over the world. The local storytelling customs and film businesses are frequently eclipsed by this widespread consumption.

- *Fast food proliferation:* The rise of fast food restaurants like McDonald's has altered eating customs and tastes throughout the world, frequently decreasing the desire for regional cuisines.

- **Implications:**
    - *Loss of Cultural Identity*: International cultural aspects may eclipse or supplant regional customs, languages, and behaviours.
    - *Experience Standardization*: People may have a more homogeneous cultural environment globally, which lessens the diversity and depth of human experiences.

12.1.2. Cultural Diversity:

- **Description:** In the digital era, cultural diversity pertains to the maintenance and commemoration of unique cultural identities and customs, enabled by digital technologies that permit the dissemination and representation of an extensive array of cultural materials.

- **Factors that Promote Cultural Diversity:**
    - *Internet accessibility*: The internet offers a global forum for the exchange of local content and a variety of cultural expressions.
    - *Digital Content Creation*: People can express their distinct cultural viewpoints through the use of content creation and sharing tools like social media, YouTube, and blogs.
    - *Virtual Communities*: People with similar cultural interests can interact and support one another through online communities and forums.

- **As an illustration:**
    - *YouTube and Independent Filmmaking*: Without depending on conventional media outlets, filmmakers from a variety of backgrounds can communicate their tales and cultural experiences on platforms such as YouTube.
    - *Socioeconomic Media Campaigns*: By drawing attention to particular cultural and socioeconomic challenges, movements like #BlackLivesMatter and #MeToo have fostered diversity and inclusivity.
    - *Language Preservation Apps:* By making endangered languages available to a worldwide audience, apps and websites devoted to language study and preservation (like Duolingo and Memrise) contribute to the survival of these languages.

- **Implications:**
    - *Increased Cultural Awareness:* Being exposed to a variety of cultures can help one comprehend and value the various customs and viewpoints of other cultures.
    - *Empowerment of Marginalized Communities:* Underrepresented communities may share their stories and fight for their rights thanks to digital channels, which give them a voice.
    - *Innovation and Creativity*: New forms of creative and cultural expression might result from the merging of many cultural influences.

12.1.3. Handling the Challenges of Cultural Homogenization and Diversity:

- **Challenges:**
    - *Dominance of Major Platforms:* By promoting

content that appeals to a worldwide audience, major digital platforms frequently marginalize local content creators.

  ○ *Digital divide* refers to the unequal access to digital technology that underprivileged populations face, with less resources available to them to communicate their cultures online.

- **Prospects:**
  ○ *Promoting Local Content*: Local content makers can receive financial assistance, training, and platforms that highlight their culture from governments and groups.
  ○ *Inclusive Technology Policies:* Promoting cultural diversity and bridging the digital divide can be achieved by guaranteeing equal access to digital technology.

- **Instances of Equilibrium Attempts:**
  ○ *UNESCO's Digital Heritage Initiatives:* With the use of digital technologies, historical items can be digitally preserved and cultural heritage can be promoted through online cultural education programs, among other projects.
  ○ *National Content Platforms:* Nations like China have created their own digital ecosystems (like WeChat and TikTok/Douyin) that support regional material in addition to international influences.

In summary, the digital era offers chances as well as obstacles for cultural variety and uniformity. Global connectedness offers significant instruments for the preservation and promotion of a variety of cultural manifestations, even though it can also result in a more homogenous cultural landscape. Societies can achieve a balance between embracing global cultural influences and maintaining the depth of regional customs and identities by carefully utilizing digital technologies. Fostering a digital environment that respects and celebrates cultural diversity while acknowledging the risk of cultural homogenization requires an understanding of this relationship.

12.2. The Role of Information Technology in Cultural Exchange

In the digital age, information technology (IT) is essential for promoting and facilitating cross-cultural exchange. IT has changed how cultures interact and affect one another by bringing people together from all over the world and offering venues for sharing and experiencing a wide range of cultural expressions. This is a thorough analysis of the function of IT in cross-cultural communication with striking instances.

12.2.1. Global Communication and Connectivity:

- **Description:** Technology facilitates instantaneous communication and connectedness between people and groups globally, dismantling geographical barriers and promoting cross-cultural interchange.
- **As an illustration:**
    - *Social media platforms*, such as Facebook, Instagram, and Twitter, enable individuals to communicate with a worldwide audience about cultural experiences, customs, and viewpoints. People exchange images, films, and narratives, for instance, during cultural holidays like Chinese New Year or Diwali, to inform and interest others about these festivities.
    - *Video Conferencing Tools:* Programs like international student exchanges, virtual museum tours, and international conferences where participants share cultural perspectives are made possible by platforms like Zoom, Microsoft Teams, and Skype.

12.2.2. Generation and Distribution of Digital Content:

- **Description:** IT gives people and groups the means to produce and distribute digital information, opening up their culture to a wider audience.
- **As an illustration:**
  - *YouTube:* This site for sharing videos is a vital conduit for cross-cultural communication. Videos about other cultures' daily lives, music, food, and customs are uploaded by content creators from around the world, reaching millions of people globally. Through music videos and entertainment programs, channels like T-Series (India) and KBS World TV (South Korea) provide viewers with insights into their different cultures.
  - *Sites for Blogging:* People publish blogs on websites like Medium and WordPress where they discuss their cultural experiences, customs, and ancestry. Travel bloggers frequently share their experiences learning about and appreciating other cultures throughout the globe through their documentation.

12.2.3. Resources for Online Education and Learning

- **Description:** IT makes it possible to access learning materials and virtual classrooms that support language learning and cross-cultural comprehension.
- **As an illustration:**
  - *Coursera and edX:* These virtual learning environments include classes on global cultures, languages, and historical subjects, frequently in association with academic institutions. For instance, students worldwide may be able to access courses on traditional Japanese arts, cuisine, and social norms in a course on Japanese culture.

○ *Apps for language learning:* Duolingo, Rosetta Stone, and Babbel assist users in learning new languages and promote understanding and communication across cultural boundaries. Learning a new language helps people understand the culture that it is linked with, which promotes improved understanding and communication.

12.2.4. Augmented and Virtual Reality

- **Description:** Through virtual and augmented reality, IT provides immersive experiences that let people engage in interactive cultural exploration.
- **As an illustration:**
    ○ *Google Arts & Culture:* This platform offers virtual tours of museums, historical places, and cultural icons all over the world using virtual reality technology. Users can experience art and history from many civilizations by visiting the Louvre in Paris or the Uffizi Gallery in Florence from the comfort of their own homes.
    ○ *VR Cultural Experiences*: Apps like Oculus VR and HTC Vive provide deeply immersive cultural experiences by allowing users to stroll through ancient Rome or see a traditional African hamlet.

12.2.5. Digital Preservation of Cultural Heritage:

- **Description:** Technology plays a crucial role in digitizing and protecting cultural content so that future generations and a worldwide audience can access it.
- **As an illustration:**
    ○ *Europeana* is a digital portal that offers millions of

digitized artefacts from European galleries, museums, archives, and libraries. It preserves Europe's cultural legacy by containing books, music, films, and artwork.

- *Smithsonian Digitization Program:* The Smithsonian Institution makes artefacts from its extensive collections accessible online for study and instruction by digitizing them. Anybody with an internet connection can view everything from historical papers to indigenous art.

12.2.6. Campaigns and Movements on Social Media:

- **Description:** IT enables social media campaigns and movements that draw attention to cultural issues and develop solidarity and cultural awareness.
- **As an illustration:**
    - The *#BlackLivesMatter* movement has garnered substantial traction on social media, drawing attention to concerns of cultural identity and racial inequity on a global scale. It has spurred debates and protests around the globe, advancing awareness of and support for African American rights and culture.
    - *#MeToo:* Originally a campaign against sexual harassment and assault, #MeToo has expanded to include cultural dimensions of gender relations and has given women worldwide the confidence to share their experiences, so promoting a global conversation on cultural norms and gender equality.

12.2.7. Cultural Festivals and Events Online:

- **Description:** People may virtually experience and enjoy many cultures thanks to IT, which also makes it possible to organize and participate in online cultural festivals and events.

- **As an illustration:**
    - The annual *Global Citizen Festival* is an online music festival that showcases international musicians and encourages social activism and cultural knowledge. It celebrates world culture by bringing together a varied range of musical artists and listeners.
    - *Virtual Cultural Exchange Programs*: Initiatives such as AFS Intercultural Programs provide students with online opportunities to engage in culturally-sensitive activities including language exchanges, cooking workshops, and virtual homestays.

Role of IT in Cultural Exchange

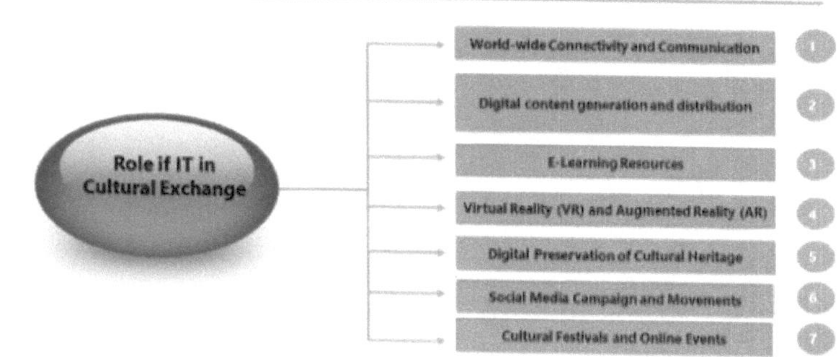

Source: The Sociology of Information Technology; GoodMan Series; (Patrick Mukosha 2024).

Figure 3: The Role of Information Technology in Cultural Exchange

In summary, Cultural exchange has been significantly impacted by information technology, which has made it simpler than ever to share, engage with, and value the diversity of cultures. IT creates a more globally linked and culturally conscious world through global connectivity, digital content creation, online learning, virtual reality, digital preservation, social media movements, and online cultural events. Gaining knowledge of and using these IT capabilities can improve cross-cultural communication.

12.3. Digital Media and Cultural Hegemony

Digital media has a significant influence on how knowledge and culture are disseminated, influencing how cultures see themselves and one another. Through the use of digital platforms, dominant cultures impose their values, beliefs, and behaviors on less dominant cultures, a phenomenon known as cultural hegemony. In order to handle the complexity of cultural dynamics in the digital era, an IT specialist must have a thorough awareness of the mechanics of digital media and cultural hegemony, as well as their repercussions.

12.3.1. Comprehending Cultural Hegemony:

- **Description:** The term "cultural hegemony" describes how the worldview of the ruling class, which eventually becomes the acknowledged cultural norm, dominates a society with a varied population. Antonio Gramsci presented this idea, which also applies to how digital media upholds the worldwide domination of particular civilizations.
- **Mechanisms:**
    - *Content Control:* A sizable amount of media content worldwide is created and maintained by dominant civilizations.
    Platform Dominance: Major digital platforms are frequently owned and operated by organizations from prevailing cultures.
    - *Economic Power*: Dominant cultures are able to invest more in the creation and dissemination of media due to economic imbalances.

12.3.2. International Media Outlets and Cultural Hegemony:

- **Description:** Popular US-based digital media platforms such as YouTube, Netflix, Facebook, and Twitter are products of Western ideology and values.
- **As an illustration:**
  - *Netflix:* Netflix is a global streaming service with a huge selection of content, most of which is created in the United States. Television series such as "Stranger Things" and "House of Cards" serve as global ambassadors for American cultural ideals and societal conventions, in addition to providing entertainment.
  - *YouTube:* With its US headquarters, YouTube heavily favours video created by American creators. Viral content and trends frequently mirror American cultural norms, affecting viewers worldwide.
- **Implications:**
  - *Cultural Uniformity*: When content from dominant cultures is widely consumed, it can homogenize global culture and obscure regional customs and identities.
  - *Diminished Visibility of Local Content*: Content that deviates from prevailing cultural norms and local artists may be marginalized by algorithms that prefer popular content.

12.3.3. Description of Media Production and Economic Power:

- **Description:** Rich nations make significant investments in media production, enabling them to provide excellent material that is widely viewed and consumed around the world.

- **As an illustration:**
    - *Hollywood Films*: One of the best examples of cultural hegemony is the international success of Hollywood films. In addition to ruling global box offices, blockbusters like "Avengers: Endgame" and "Avatar" also promote American cultural ideals, storylines, and lifestyles.
    - *Apple and Google:* As the two biggest tech giants, they influence how people use the internet by prioritizing Western apps and content in their ecosystems (i.e., iOS, Android, App Store, Google Play).

- **Implications:**
    - *Cultural exportation* is the process by which dominant cultures use popular media to spread their beliefs and ideals, affecting people's attitudes and actions all across the world.
    - *Local Market Displacement:* Local media industries may be eclipsed by content from dominating cultures with higher production quality and marketing resources.

12.3.4. The Impact of Social Media on Cultural Norms

- **Description:** Social networking sites encourage particular kinds of interactions and content, which in turn shapes societal norms and habits.
- **As an illustration:**
    - *Instagram Influencers*: A large number of prominent Instagram users uphold Western standards of lifestyle, fashion, and beauty. Global trends are

influenced by their enormous fan bases, frequently at the expense of regional cultural expressions.

- *Facebook Algorithms*: Popular and engaging information, frequently created in dominant cultures, is frequently promoted by Facebook's content algorithms, which has an impact on conversations and social norms around the world.

- **Implications:**
  - *Global Conformity*: Social media has the potential to cause a global convergence of cultural norms, displacing regional customs and values with those of prevailing civilizations.
  - *Cultural Misrepresentation*: Stereotypes and inaccurate depictions of other cultures can result from the predominance of particular cultural narratives.

12.3.5. Countering Cultural Hegemony:

- **Strategies:**
  - *Promoting Local Content*: To counteract the influence of dominant cultures, local content creation and distribution are encouraged.
  - *Policy Regulation*: Governments have the authority to enact laws that encourage domestic media companies and control the hegemony of foreign media.
  - *Digital literacy:* Improving users' ability to interact critically with media information and identify a range of cultural expressions.

- **As an illustration:**
  - *China's Media Regulation*: To protect and advance Chinese culture, China imposes stringent laws on

foreign media and encourages the creation of local material on websites like WeChat and Douyin, which is China's version of TikTok.

- *European Audiovisual Media Services Directive (AVMSD):* To support the richness of European culture, the EU mandates that streaming services guarantee that a minimum of thirty percent of their material is generated domestically.

12.3.6. Technology's Contribution to Fostering Cultural Diversity

- **Description:** Technology can support cultural hegemony through digital media, but it can also be used to promote cultural variety and preserve regional traditions.
- **As an illustration:**
    - *Digital Archives*: Wide-ranging cultural artefact collections are digitized and made available through platforms such as Europeana and the Internet Archive, guaranteeing the preservation and accessibility of a diversified cultural heritage.
    - *Crowdsourcing Cultural Content:* To create a more comprehensive portrayal of world cultures, sites such as Wikipedia rely on user contributions to document and share knowledge about other civilizations.
- **Implications:**
    - *Cultural Empowerment:* By enabling underrepresented cultures to communicate their histories and customs, technology can challenge the dominance of dominant civilizations.
    - *Enhanced Cultural Awareness*: Having access to a variety of cultural content can help people appreciate and comprehend other cultures on a global scale.

In summary, through global platforms, economic power, and social media influence, digital media greatly amplifies the reach and impact of dominant cultures, hence contributing to cultural hegemony. Technology does, however, also offer ways to mitigate these impacts, such as through encouraging local content, putting supportive laws into place, and raising digital literacy. Through comprehension of these relationships, we may use IT to promote a more varied and equitable cultural environment in the digital era.

Chapter 13: Environmental Impacts and Information Technology

13.1. E-Waste and Electronic Recycling

Discarded electrical or electronic equipment is referred to as "e-waste," or electronic garbage. The lifespan of electronic items shortens as technology progresses quickly, increasing the amount of e-waste produced. Managing this expanding waste stream and reducing its negative effects on the environment and public health require effective electronic recycling. This is a comprehensive guide to electronic recycling and e-waste, complete with real-world examples.

13.1.1. Comprehending the Description of E-Waste: Description:

- **Description:** Products that have reached the end of their useful lives, such as computers, televisions, cellphones, printers, and household appliances, are all included in the category of e-waste.
- **Components:** In addition to dangerous compounds like lead, mercury, and cadmium, e-waste also contains valuable materials like gold, silver, copper, and platinum.
- **As an illustration:**
    - *Smartphones:* The technology behind smartphones is advancing quickly, and regular updates add a lot of e-waste. For example, a lot of customers switch out their phones every two to three years.
    - *Televisions:* Many outdated CRT televisions are being thrown away as a result of the switch from cathode-ray tube (CRT) to flat-screen devices.

13.1.2. The Effects of E-Waste on the Environment and Human Health:

- **Environmental Impacts:**
  - *Pollution:* Air, water, and soil pollution results from improper e-waste disposal. Water supplies can get contaminated by toxic compounds that seep into the ground.
  - *Depletion of Resources:* Valuable metals found in e-waste contribute to the depletion of natural resources if they are not recycled.
- **Health Impacts:**
  - *Toxic Exposure:* Breathing difficulties, brain damage, and cancer are just a few of the serious health problems that can result from being exposed to dangerous chemicals from e-waste.
- **As an illustration:**
  - *Guiyu, China:* Known as the "e-waste capital of the world," impromptu e-waste recycling methods have caused serious environmental damage and health issues for the locals.

13.1.3. Methods for Recycling Electronics

- **Description:** In electronic recycling, hazardous components are disposed of safely while valuable elements are extracted from e-waste and disassembled, processed, and recovered.
- **Procedures:**
  - *Collecting:* Drop-off locations, take-back initiatives, and e-waste collecting events are used to gather e-waste from individuals, companies, and organizations.
  - *Disassembly:* Circuit boards, batteries, and plastics are separated from other parts of the device by hand.
  - *Shredding:* Electronic waste is reduced in size by mechanical shredders and subsequently separated

into many material categories.

- *Material Recovery:* Valuable metals and materials are recovered using sophisticated processes like smelting, eddy current separation, and magnetic separation.

- **As an illustration:**
  - *Dell Reconnect Program:* Dell and Goodwill Industries collaborate to gather and recycle used devices, offering customers convenient drop-off locations and guaranteeing ecologically friendly recycling.
  - *Apple's Daisy Robot:* Apple effectively disassembles iPhones using Daisy, a robot designed to retrieve valuable components like aluminium, tungsten, and rare earth elements.

13.1.4. International E-Waste Management Initiatives:

- **Laws and Policies:**
  - The Waste Electrical and Electronic Equipment Directive (*WEEE Directive*) of the European Union requires its member states to put in place mechanisms for the recovery, recycling, and collection of electronic waste. The cost of treating and discarding their products must be covered by the producers.
  - *Extended Producer Responsibility (EPR):* Laws in South Korea and Japan mandate that manufacturers return and recycle their goods, which encourages the development of environmentally friendly electronics.
- **Global Cooperation:**
  - *Basel Convention:* An international agreement aimed at ensuring ecologically responsible handling of e-waste and minimizing the transfer of hazardous

waste between countries, especially industrialized and developing nations.

- **As an illustration:**
  - *SWICO Recycling:* The Swiss Association for Information, Communication, and Organizational Technology (SWICO) oversees a very effective e-waste recycling system in Switzerland that guarantees both high recycling rates and secure disposal.
  - *India's Regulations for the Management of E-Waste:* These regulations mandate that producers gather a specific portion of the e-waste produced by their goods and make sure that it is recycled properly.

13.1.5. Difficulties with E-Waste Management:

- **Difficulties:**
  - *Informal Recycling:* Unsafe procedures are used by informal recyclers in many poor nations to process e-waste, posing a risk to human health and the environment.
  - *Lack of Knowledge:* Improper handling and disposal of e-waste might result from consumers' frequent ignorance of the correct recycling and disposal practices.
  - *Complexity of Devices:* Recycling modern electronic devices can be costly and difficult due to their complicated design and mixture of components.
- **As an illustration:**
  - *Agbogbloshie, Ghana:* One of the biggest unofficial e-waste recycling locations, where employees disassemble devices without safety gear, posing serious risks to their health and the environment.
  - *Lack of Infrastructure:* In many areas, efficient e-waste

management is hampered by the absence of sufficient recycling infrastructure and services.

13.1.6. Prospects and Novelties in E-Waste Recycling

- **Innovative Remedies:**
    - *Urban Mining:* Compared to traditional mining, extracting valuable metals from e-waste using cutting-edge recycling technologies can be more effective and environmentally beneficial.
    - *Design for Recycling:* Encourage manufacturers to create products that are simpler to disassemble and recycle in order to enhance the management of electronic waste.
- **As an illustration:**
    - *Fairphone:* A smartphone that promotes durability and recyclability by having modular parts that are simple to repair or replace.
    - *International Recyclers of Electronics (ERI):* ERI efficiently recycles e-waste and recovers precious metals through the use of cutting-edge shredding and separation technology.

In summary, in the digital age, e-waste and electronic recycling are important problems with substantial effects on the environment, human health, and economy. To reduce the harmful effects of electronic waste and advance a sustainable future, effective management of e-waste through ethical recycling methods, supportive legislation, and creative solutions is crucial. Ongoing initiatives to enhance e-waste management and recycling will be essential in tackling this as technology develops further.

13.2. Energy Consumption of Information Technologies

With the exponential growth in demand for digital services, information technology' (IT) energy usage is becoming a crucial concern. IT uses a lot of energy, from data centers that power the internet to individual devices and the Internet of Things' (IoT) explosion of connected devices. This thorough discussion explores the different aspects of IT energy use and is backed up by striking examples.

13.2.1. **Data Centres:**

- **Description:** Computer systems and related parts, including storage and telecommunications, are housed in data centres. They are essential for handling, distributing, and storing vast volumes of data.
- **Energy Consumption:** Because servers, storage devices, and networking equipment need to be powered by large amounts of electricity, data centres are extremely energy-intensive. They also require powerful cooling systems to avoid overheating.
- **As an illustration:**
  - *Google Data Centres:* Although the firm has committed to utilize renewable energy to counteract this, Google's data centres require enormous quantities of electricity. Google declared in 2020 that it has achieved four years in a row of matching its energy use with 100% renewable energy.
  - *Facebook's Prineville Data Centre*: This data centre, which is situated in Oregon, has energy-efficient server designs and use cutting-edge cooling methods including evaporative cooling to lessen its carbon footprint.

- **Measures of Energy Efficiency:**
    - *Virtualisation:* By enabling several virtual servers to operate on a single physical server, virtualization lowers the need for actual servers.
    - *Advanced Cooling Solutions:* By utilizing natural airflows, methods like liquid cooling and free cooling lessen the need for conventional air conditioning systems.
    - *Integration of Renewable Energy:* To power their data centres, many businesses are investing in renewable energy sources including solar and wind power.

13.2.2. Personal Devices

- **Description:** Personal devices, which are now commonplace in daily life, include laptops, desktop computers, tablets, and smartphones.
- **Energy Consumption:** Despite the fact that individual devices only require little quantities of energy, the combined effect of their widespread use is substantial.
- **As an illustration:**
    - *Smartphones:* The annual charging consumption of a common smartphone is between 2 and 7 kWh. With billions of cellphones in use worldwide, this may seem insignificant, but the overall energy usage is significant.
    - *Desktops vs. Laptops:* In general, laptops use less energy than desktop computers. A desktop computer can require up to 300 watts when in use, whereas a normal laptop only uses 20 to 50 watts.
- **Measures of Energy Efficiency:**
    - *Energy Star Certification:* The Energy Star certification is given to products that satisfy specific

energy efficiency requirements. With the use of this service, shoppers can find products that use less energy.

- ○ *Features of Power Management:* Power-saving modes are built into a lot of contemporary electronics, which lower energy consumption when the device is idle.

13.2.3. Internet of Things (IoT):

- **Description:** The term "internet of things" (IoT) describes a system of linked devices that may communicate and share data. These gadgets include everything from industrial sensors to smart home appliances.
- **Energy Consumption:** Depending on the kind and use, Internet of Things devices have quite different energy footprints. Even though individual Internet of Things devices usually only use a little amount of energy, the sheer quantity of devices might result in a large cumulative energy consumption.
- **As an illustration:**
  - ○ *Smart Home Appliances:* Appliances that maximize energy efficiency in houses include lights, security systems, and thermostats. For instance, by recognizing user patterns and modifying temperatures appropriately, a smart thermostat can lower the amount of energy used for heating and cooling.
  - ○ *Industrial Internet of Things (IoT):* IoT sensors in industrial settings keep an eye on equipment and streamline processes to save energy. For example, IoT-based predictive maintenance can stop equipment breakdowns, saving downtime and energy.

- **Measures of Energy Efficiency:**
  - *Low-Power Protocols:* To reduce energy consumption, Internet of Things devices frequently employ low-power communication protocols including LoRaWAN, Z-Wave, and Zigbee.
  - *Energy Harvesting:* To lessen their need on conventional power sources, some Internet of Things devices employ energy harvesting strategies, such as using solar or kinetic energy, to power themselves.

13.2.4. Mining Cryptocurrencies

- **Description:** Verifying transactions and entering them into the blockchain ledger are part of cryptocurrency mining. Significant computational power and energy are needed for this process.
- **Energy Consumption**: Because mining cryptocurrencies, especially Bitcoin, requires a lot of complicated calculations, it consumes a lot of energy. The amount of energy used just for Bitcoin mining is comparable to whole nations.
- **As an illustration:**
  - *Bitcoin Mining:* As of 2021, the yearly energy consumption of Bitcoin mining was approximately 121 terawatt-hours (TWh), which is equivalent to the energy consumption of a medium-sized nation like Argentina.
  - *Ethereum's Shift to Proof of Stake:* Another well-known cryptocurrency, Ethereum, has been shifting from a proof-of-work (PoW) to a proof-of-stake (PoS) model. By doing away with the requirement for a lot of processing power, the PoS model dramatically lowers energy usage.
- **Measures of Energy Efficiency:**

- *Hardware Efficiency:* Energy consumption can be decreased by using mining hardware that is more energy-efficient, such as Application-Specific Integrated Circuits (ASICs).
- *Renewable Energy:* In order to power their operations sustainably, some mining enterprises are situating themselves close to renewable energy sources.

13.2.5. Telecommunications Networks:

- **Description:** Global communication and information sharing are made possible by telecommunications networks, which include cellular networks and the internet infrastructure.
- **Energy Consumption:** Considering the requirement to power base stations, data transmission devices, and network infrastructure, telecommunications networks use a significant amount of energy.
- **As an illustration:**
  - *5G Networks:* The introduction of 5G technology brings with it the promise of increased capacity and quicker speeds, but it also presents energy efficiency challenges. In contrast to 4G, 5G networks are intended to use less energy per unit of data sent.
  - *Undersea cables:* The foundation of the world wide web, these cables require a lot of energy to operate and maintain. As an illustration, the Marea cable, which crosses the Atlantic Ocean, is an essential piece of infrastructure that needs continuous electricity supply.
- **Measures of Energy Efficiency:**
  - *Network Optimization:* Energy utilization in

telecommunications networks can be optimized by methods like network virtualization and dynamic power management.

- *Energy-Efficient Protocols:* By putting energy-efficient networking protocols into place, data transmission power requirements can be decreased.

13.2.6. New Innovations and Solutions

- **Eco-friendly Data Centres:**
  - *Microsoft's Project Natick* is an experimental data centre that is submerged and uses the ocean's natural cooling capabilities to use less energy.
  - *The Arctic Data Centre of Facebook:* This data centre, which is in Luleå, Sweden, uses the chilly weather to naturally cool servers, which uses a lot less electricity.
- **Machine Learning and Artificial Intelligence**: Energy consumption in IT infrastructure can be optimized with AI and machine learning. Google, for instance, saves a lot of energy by using AI to control the cooling systems in its data centres.
- **Edge Computing**: Edge computing saves energy by processing data closer to its source, hence minimizing the need for long-distance data transmission.

In summary, with the growth of digital services, information technology energy consumption is becoming a major challenge. Energy consumption from IT infrastructure, ranging from data centers and personal devices to Internet of Things and cryptocurrency mining, has an effect on the environment. However, the IT industry can lessen its energy footprint by using creative solutions, energy-efficient designs, and a move toward renewable energy sources. It is imperative to comprehend and tackle these obstacles in order to foster lasting advancements in technology.

13.3. Sustainable Solutions for Mitigating Environmental Impact

Information Technology (IT) has a large environmental impact because of the energy it uses, the e-waste it produces, and the resources it uses. To lessen these effects, there are a lot of sustainable options available. These remedies include everything from energy-efficient hardware and green data centers to software optimization and e-waste recycling programs. Here is a detailed description of these environmentally friendly options, backed up by striking instances.

13.3.1. Green Data Centres:

- **Description:** Green data centres use renewable energy sources and increase energy efficiency to reduce their negative environmental effects.
- **Important Techniques:**
    - *Energy-Efficient Cooling:* involves lowering the amount of energy needed for cooling by utilizing cutting-edge methods including liquid cooling, hot/cold aisle confinement, and free cooling.
    - *Energy from Renewable Sources:* Using hydroelectric, solar, and wind power to power data centres.
- **As an illustration:**
    - *Google's Data Centres:* By 2030, Google plans to run its data centres entirely on carbon-free energy sources around-the-clock. Google has made investments in renewable energy projects to power its facilities and employs cutting edge AI to manage cooling.
    - *Facebook's Luleå Data Centre* is one of the world's most energy-efficient data centres. It is situated in Sweden and makes use of the country's naturally

chilly environment for effective cooling. Hydroelectric power also powers the data centre.

13.3.2. Energy-Efficient Hardware:

- **Description:** Reducing IT's environmental impact requires developing and utilizing hardware that uses less energy while maintaining or increasing performance.
- **Important Techniques:**
    - *Low-Power Components*: Making use of parts with low power consumption, such as memory, CPUs, and storage units.
    - *Features for Power Management:* Using sleep modes, power gating, and dynamic voltage scaling to cut down on energy consumption when not in use.
- **As an illustration:**
    - *Apple's M1 processor*: Designed to provide excellent performance with low power consumption, the M1 processor is found in the company's most recent MacBooks and iPads. This results in much longer battery life and lower energy use.
    - *ARM CPUs:* Known for their superior energy efficiency over conventional x86 CPUs, ARM processors are found in a large number of smartphones and embedded devices.

13.3.3. Optimization of Software

- **Description:** By optimizing the utilization of hardware resources, efficient software can dramatically lower the energy consumption of information technology systems.
- **Important Techniques:** Writing code that reduces resource consumption and maximizes processing effectiveness is

known as efficient coding.

The adoption of virtualization and containerization can optimize resource allocation and minimize the need for physical servers.

- **As an illustration:**
    - *TensorFlow by Google*: An open-source machine learning library that has been energy-efficiently improved, enabling AI applications to operate more smoothly on a range of hardware.
    - *Docker Containers:* By enabling the execution of programs in isolated containers, Docker enhances resource efficiency by enabling the low- overhead deployment of numerous apps on a single server.

13.3.4. Renewable Energy Integration:

- **Description:** Reducing the carbon footprint associated with electricity use can be achieved by integrating renewable energy sources into IT processes.
- **Important Techniques:**
    - *On-Site renewable Energy Generation:* Installing solar panels, wind turbines, or other renewable energy systems on-site to power IT equipment is known as "on-site renewable energy generation."
    - *Purchasing Renewable Energy Credits (RECs):* Acquiring RECs will help the renewable energy market and offset energy consumption.
- **As an illustration:**
    - *Microsoft's Renewable Energy Initiatives:* The company is dedicated to becoming carbon negative by 2030 and has been acquiring renewable energy to offset the energy used in its data centres.
    - *AWS, or Amazon Web Services:* To power its data

centres with renewable energy, AWS has a number of renewable energy projects, including as wind and solar farms.

13.3.5. Recycling E-Waste and the Circular Economy

- **Description:** Reducing the negative effects of abandoned electronic equipment on the environment is possible through encouraging a circular economy and treating electronic trash properly.
- **Important Techniques:**
    - *E-Waste Recycling Programs:* Programs for the collection, recycling, and appropriate disposal of e-waste are established.
    - *Product Lifecycle Extension:* Creating long-lasting, repairable, and upgradable items helps prolong their lifespan and cut down on waste.
    - *Material Recovery:* Extracting useful components from electronic waste so they can be repurposed in fresh goods.
- **As an illustration:**
    - *Dell's Closed-Loop Recycling:* This program reduces the demand for virgin resources by gathering obsolete electronics, removing valuable elements, and repurposing them in new products.
    - *Apple's Daisy Robot:* To encourage recycling and cut down on e-waste, Apple utilizes the Daisy robot to disassemble iPhones and recover precious materials.

13.3.6. Virtualization and Cloud Computing

- **Description:** Technologies like virtualization and cloud computing can lessen the environmental effect of IT operations while also increasing resource utilization.

- **Important Techniques:**
  - *Resource Pulling:* In a cloud setting, resource pooling is the practice of pooling resources to maximize use and minimize the need for surplus capacity.
  - *Scalable Infrastructure:* Reducing energy waste by using scalable cloud infrastructure to modify resource usage in response to demand.

- **As an illustration:**
  - *Elastic Compute Cloud (EC2) from Amazon Web Services (AWS):* EC2 enables users to adjust computer capacity in response to demand, maximizing resource use and energy savings.
  - *Google Cloud Platform:* To manage workloads and lower energy usage, Google's cloud services make use of highly efficient data centres and cutting-edge AI.

13.3.7. Development of Green Software

- **Description:** creating software with a lifecycle that prioritizes sustainability and energy efficiency.

- **Important Techniques:**
  - *Eco-Design concepts:* To reduce energy consumption and environmental effect, incorporate eco-design concepts into the software development process.
  - *Energy-Efficient Algorithms:* Creating algorithms that optimize for energy efficiency without sacrificing functionality is known as "energy-efficient algorithm development."

- **As an illustration:**
  - *organizations for Green Coding:* The Green Software Foundation, for example, encourages developers to write software with as little environmental impact

as possible. Other organizations also support green coding methods.

In summary, a holistic strategy is needed to mitigate the environmental impact of IT, including creative data center designs, energy-efficient hardware and software, integration of renewable energy sources, and efficient e-waste disposal. The IT sector can greatly lessen its environmental impact while still meeting the rising demand for digital services by implementing these sustainable solutions. In the digital age, putting these tactics into practice and growing them will be essential to long-term viability.

Chapter 14: Ethical Considerations in Information Technology

14.1. Ethical Issues in Data Collection and Use

Many facets of contemporary life depend on the gathering and use of data, which spurs innovation and informs choices across many sectors of the economy. But these actions also bring up serious ethical issues, especially when it comes to consent, privacy, data security, and the possibility of abuse. Understanding and addressing these ethical challenges is crucial for IT professionals in order to guarantee acceptable data practices. Here's a detailed explanation that, when feasible, includes colorful examples.

14.1.1. Privacy Issues:

- **Description:** When personal information is gathered, kept, and utilized without people's knowledge or beyond their reasonable expectations, privacy issues can occur.
- **Important Concerns:**
    - *Surveillance:* Privacy may be violated by the widespread tracking of people using technologies like CCTV, location data, and internet activity tracking.
    - *Data breaches:* Unauthorized access to personal information can result in serious consequences, such as financial loss, shame, and identity theft.
- **As an illustration:**
    - *The Facebook-Cambridge Analytica scandal (2018):* It was discovered that the data mining company had taken millions of Facebook users' personal information without their knowledge or permission and had used it for political advertising. The dangers of data misuse and the requirement for strict data protection measures were brought to light by this

occurrence.

- *Google Street View:* The company acknowledged in 2010 that personal information had unintentionally been gathered by its Street View vehicles from unencrypted Wi-Fi networks. Significant privacy issues regarding inadvertent data acquisition were brought up by this occurrence.

14.1.2. Transparency and Consent:

- **Description:** In order to gather data ethically, people must give their express, informed consent, attesting to the fact that they understand what data is being collected, how it will be used, and who will receive it.
- **Important Concerns:**
    - *Informed Consent:* Users must freely give their consent after being fully informed about data collection procedures. Long and intricate privacy policies, however, frequently obstruct genuine informed consent.
    - *Transparency:* Businesses need to be open and honest about their data practices, including the types of data they gather, why they collect it, and how long they plan to keep it.
- **As an illustration:**
    - *GDPR Compliance:* Before collecting personal data from users, enterprises are required by the General Data Protection Regulation (GDPR) of the European Union to seek explicit agreement from those users. Clear communication regarding data practices is also necessary. For example, in order to comply with GDPR, websites frequently display cookie consent banners.

- *App Tracking Transparency* was introduced by Apple with the iOS update, which mandates that apps obtain the consent of the user before tracking their activity on websites and applications owned by other firms.

14.1.3. Data Security:

- **Description:** To stop misuse, illegal access, and breaches, it is essential to ensure the security of data that has been gathered. Implementing organizational and technical safeguards to shield data from dangers is known as data security.
- **Important Concerns:**
    - *Encryption:* Data is encrypted in order to prevent unwanted access.
    - *Access Controls:* Restricting authorized personnel's access to data.
    - *Incident Response:* Having strong procedures in place to react quickly and efficiently to data breaches is known as incident response.
- **As an illustration:**
    - *Data Breach at Equifax*: A significant data breach at Equifax in 2017 resulted in the exposure of 147 million people's personal data. Robust data security measures are necessary, as the intrusion was ascribed to inadequate security protocols.
    - *Health Insurance Portability and Accountability Act (HIPAA)*: Healthcare providers must have robust data security measures in place in order to comply with HIPAA, which establishes requirements for the protection of health information in the US.

14.1.4. Discrimination and Bias

- **Description:** If data collection and utilization are not done with caution, bias and discrimination may be reinforced or made worse. Applications involving machine learning (ML) and artificial intelligence (AI) are especially prone to this problem.
- **Important Concerns:**
    - *Bias in Data:* The results of algorithms trained on pre-existing data sets are likely to reinforce pre-existing prejudices.
    - *Discriminatory Outcomes*: Automated systems have the potential to provide discriminatory outcomes in the legal, lending, employing, and healthcare sectors, among other areas.
- **As an illustration:**
    - *Amazon's AI Recruiting Tool:* The AI tool, which was trained on resumes submitted to the company over a ten-year period, the majority of which came from men, shown bias against women. As a result, Amazon cancelled it.
    - *Predictive policing:* It has been said that certain algorithms used in predictive policing unfairly target communities of colour, resulting in biased law enforcement actions.

14.1.5. Restrictions on Use and Minimization of Data

- **Description:** Only gathering the information required for a certain goal and refraining from utilizing it for unrelated purposes without further consent are aspects of ethical data collection.
- **Important Concerns:**
    - *Limitation on Use:* Information must be gathered for a specified, authorized purpose and must not be used

for other purposes without permission.

Data minimization: Information should only be gathered and stored insofar as it is required for the intended use.

- **As an illustration:**
  - *Google Fit and Health Data:* In order to deliver fitness insights, Google Fit gathers health data from its customers. If this information was utilized for unrelated purposes—like targeted advertising—without the users' consent, ethical questions might surface.
  - *Apps for Contact Tracing:* Several nations created contact tracing applications during the COVID-19 pandemic. These apps had to follow ethical data collection guidelines, gathering only the information essential to monitor virus exposure and make sure it wasn't misused.

14.1.6. Governance and Accountability

- **Description:** In order to supervise the ethical gathering and use of data, organizations need to be held responsible for their data practices and have governance mechanisms in place.
- **Important Concerns:**
  - *Data governance* is the establishment of roles, processes, and guidelines for the moral and secure management of data.
  - *Accountability:* Ensuring that regulatory supervision and audits are in place to hold companies responsible for their data activities.
- **As an illustration:**
  - *Facebook Oversight Board:* To ensure accountability and openness in decision-making, Facebook created

an independent Oversight Board in response to complaints regarding its content moderation policies.

Officers for Data Protection (DPOs): Organizations must designate a DPO in accordance with GDPR in order to supervise adherence to data protection regulations and guarantee moral data practices.

In summary, the ethical dilemmas surrounding the gathering and use of data are complex and include issues with privacy, accountability, consent and openness, bias and discrimination, data security, purpose limitation, and data minimization. Strong regulations, cutting-edge technological solutions, and a dedication to openness and user rights are all necessary to address these problems. As data becomes more and more essential to modern society, it is crucial to uphold ethical standards in data activities in order to safeguard people and foster confidence in digital systems.

14.2. Algorithmic Bias and Discrimination

When developing and implementing machine learning (ML) and artificial intelligence (AI) systems, there are important ethical concerns related to discrimination and bias in algorithms. These biases develop when algorithms generate biased results, which frequently mirror and exacerbate preexisting societal injustices. Examining these problems' causes, effects, and mitigation techniques is necessary to comprehend them.

14.2.1. Getting to Know Algorithmic Bias:

- **Description:** When an algorithm consistently generates biased results as a result of false assumptions made during the machine learning process, this is known as algorithmic bias.
- **Principal Causes:**
  - *Biased Training Data:* An algorithm will pick up on and reproduce biases seen in the data it was trained on.
  - *Representation Bias:* The algorithm may perform poorly for groups that are underrepresented in the training set.
  - *Historical Bias:* Injustices and inequalities from the past may be perpetuated by algorithms trained on historical data.
  - *Model Design:* Developer decisions, such as feature selection, can bring bias into the model.
- **As an illustration:**
  - *Facial Recognition Technology:* Research indicates that darker-skinned people have greater error rates in facial recognition systems, like those made by IBM,

Microsoft, and Amazon, than do lighter-skinned people. The erroneous training data that underrepresents faces with darker skin tones is the cause of this disparity.

- *Word Embeddings:* It has been discovered that gender bias exists in AI systems that use word embeddings. As an illustration of gender stereotypes found in the training data, the word "doctor" may be more strongly connected with male pronouns whereas the word "nurse" may be more closely related with female pronouns.

14.2.2. Algorithmic Bias Effects:

- **Description:** Using algorithms in crucial decision-making processes might lead to serious real-world repercussions due to algorithmic bias.
- **Principal Effects:**
    - *Discrimination:* When algorithms are biased, people may be treated unfairly because of their age, gender, race, or other protected traits.
    - *Loss of Trust:* Public confidence in technology and institutions can be damaged by prejudice in AI systems, whether real or perceived.
    - *Inequality:* Because biased algorithms maintain unequal access to opportunities and resources, they can exacerbate already-existing inequities.
- **As an illustration:**
    - *Predictive policing:* It has been said that algorithms utilized in Chicago and Los Angeles, among others, unfairly target communities of colour. certain algorithms make use of past crime data, which frequently exposes prejudices in law enforcement

procedures, increasing the amount of surveillance and policing in certain areas.

○ *Hiring Algorithms:* AI-based hiring tools have been utilized by some organizations, such as Amazon, to screen job candidates. Because the AI recruiting tool was trained on resumes submitted over a ten-year period, mostly from men, mirroring the male-dominated tech field, Amazon halted it after learning that it was prejudiced against women.

14.2.3. Reducing Algorithmic Prejudice:

- **Description:** A complex strategy including organizational, legal, and technical controls is needed to address algorithmic bias.

- **Important Techniques:**
    ○ *Diverse Training Data*: One way to lessen prejudice is to make sure the training data is representative of all relevant populations.
    ○ *Bias Detection and Correction*: Using methods to identify and address bias in algorithms during development and implementation is known as "bias detection and correction."
    ○ *Accountability and Transparency*: Keeping developers responsible for skewed results and promoting greater transparency in algorithmic decision-making processes.
    ○ *Inclusive Design*: In order to ensure that many viewpoints are taken into account, inclusive design involves involving diverse teams in the design and development of AI systems.

- **As an illustration:**
    ○ *The AI Fairness 360 toolkit:* was created by IBM and

is an open-source collection of measurements and algorithms for identifying and reducing bias in AI models. It aids creators in assessing and enhancing the fairness of their models.

- *Google's Model Cards:* Google unveiled Model Cards, which offer thorough documentation of machine learning models along with details on the data utilized, the models' intended applications, and their performance across various demographic categories. Users are better able to comprehend any biases and restrictions because to this transparency.

14.2.4. Frameworks for Regulation and Ethics:

- **Description:** When it comes to directing the appropriate development and application of AI systems to mitigate algorithmic bias, regulatory and ethical frameworks are essential.
- **Important Frameworks:**
  - *General Data Protection Regulation (GDPR):* The European Union's GDPR regulates automated decision-making and profiling and guarantees people's right to relevant information about the reasoning behind these procedures.
  - *Guidelines for AI Ethics:* Guidelines for ethical AI development have been developed by a number of organizations, including the IEEE and the European Commission, with an emphasis on accountability, openness, and justice.
- **As an illustration:**
  - *EU AI Act:* Designed to regulate AI systems according to risk assessments, the European Union is currently developing the AI Act. Stricter regulations

would apply to high-risk AI systems, like those used in recruiting and law enforcement, to guarantee equity and the absence of discrimination.

- *IEEE Global Initiative on Ethics of Autonomous and Intelligent Systems:* The recommendations from IEEE offer a foundation for creating systems that are morally sound.

In summary, significant ethical issues in the fields of AI and machine learning are brought on by discrimination and bias in algorithms. A complete strategy is needed to address these problems, one that includes using representative and varied training data, putting in place systems for bias detection and correction, making sure that accountability and openness are maintained, and abiding by ethical and legal standards. By adopting these measures, the IT sector may create trustworthy, equitable, and fair AI systems, reducing the possibility that preexisting biases and disparities would be reinforced.

14.3. Promoting Ethical Design and Use of Technology

Encouraging the ethical design and application of technology is essential to guaranteeing that advances in IT minimize harm while benefiting society. Technology-related ethical concerns cover a broad spectrum of topics, such as privacy, justice, responsibility, transparency, and inclusion. The comprehensive guide on promoting ethical technology design and use that follows is backed up with striking examples.

14.3.1. Privacy by Design:

- **Description:** Privacy by Design (PbD) is a method that incorporates privacy from the beginning into the design and management of networks, IT systems, and business procedures.
- **Important Ideas:**
    - *Be Proactive Rather Than Reactive:* Seek to prevent and anticipate privacy issues before they arise.
    - *Privacy as the Default Setting*: Make sure that, in any given IT system or business procedure, personal data is automatically protected.
    - *End-to-End Security:* Completely Integrate security safeguards at every stage of the data lifecycle.
- **As an illustration:**
    - *Apple's iOS:* With features like App Tracking Transparency, which mandates that apps get user consent before tracking their activity across other apps and websites, Apple integrates PbD into its iOS ecosystem.
    - *GDPR Compliance:* PbD is required by the General

Data Protection Regulation (GDPR), which requires enterprises to put in place the necessary organizational and technical safeguards to protect data privacy from the moment a system is designed.

14.3.2. Impartiality and Lack of Discrimination:

- **Description:** ensuring that people and groups are not subjected to discrimination in the design or use of technology on the basis of their gender, race, age, or other protected characteristics.
- **Important Techniques:**
    - *Bias Detection:* Using techniques and tools to identify and reduce bias in datasets and algorithms is known as bias detection.
    - *Inclusive Design:* Including diverse teams in the design process to guarantee that all points of view are taken into account and to spot any potential biases is known as inclusive design.
- **As an illustration:**
    - *Microsoft's Fairlearn Toolkit:* Microsoft created an open-source toolkit called Fairlearn to assist developers in evaluating and enhancing the fairness of their AI systems.
    - *Diverse AI Development Teams:* To identify and reduce bias in AI systems, organizations such as Google and IBM actively strive to form diverse AI development teams that bring a range of experiences and opinions to the table.

14.3.3. Explainability and Transparency

- **Description:** ensuring that consumers and stakeholders can easily understand and comprehend how technology, especially AI and machine learning systems, operates.

- **Important Techniques:**
    - *Model Cards:* Including comprehensive information on the data utilized, intended use cases, and performance metrics in the documentation of machine learning models.
    - *Explainable AI:* The goal of explainable AI is to create AI systems that can communicate their choices and actions to humans in a way that they can comprehend.

- **As an illustration:**
    - *Google's Model Cards*: Google unveiled Model Cards, which provide openness into the process of creating AI models as well as their advantages and disadvantages.
    - *Healthcare Providers Can Better Understand AI-Generated Recommendations with the Use of Explainable AI:* AI systems, like diagnostic tools, frequently incorporate explainability characteristics.

14.3.4. Governance and Accountability:

- **Description:** putting in place transparent governance and accountability mechanisms to monitor the moral development and application of technology.
- **Important Techniques:**
    - *Ethics Committees*: Establishing ethics boards or committees to supervise and direct the creation and implementation of technological projects.
    - *Audits and Impact Assessments:* Regularly carrying out audits and impact assessments to appraise the moral consequences of technology utilization.

- **As an illustration**:
    - *Facebook Oversight Board:* To encourage accountability and openness, Facebook formed an impartial Oversight Board to examine and offer recommendations on content moderation choices.
    - *Officers for Data Protection (DPOs):* Organizations must designate a DPO in accordance with GDPR in order to supervise adherence to data protection regulations and guarantee moral data practices.

14.3.5. Design with Users in Mind:

- **Description**: making sure that technology improves user experience and well-being by designing it with an emphasis on human needs, preferences, and values.
- **Important Techniques**:
    - *Human-Cantered Design:* Using design thinking techniques that give users' requirements and experiences top priority during the development process is known as "human-cantered design."
    - *Feedback systems:* To consistently collect user feedback and make incremental improvements, implement strong feedback systems.
- **As an illustration:**
    - *IDEO:* IDEO is a global design business that uses the principles of human-cantered design to develop creative solutions that meet actual user demands. These solutions range from digital tools to healthcare items.
    - *Customer Feedback in Software Development:* To make sure that their products satisfy customer needs and expectations, companies such as Adobe and Microsoft include user feedback into their software

development cycles.

14.3.6. Ethical Frameworks for AI

- **Description:** creating and upholding moral AI frameworks that specify guidelines and best practices for the conscientious creation and application of AI systems.
- **Important Frameworks:**
    - *The Asilomar AI Principles* are a set of 23 guidelines created by ethicists and AI researchers to direct the creation of useful AI.
    - *IEEE Global Autonomous and Intelligent Systems Ethics Initiative:* gives principles for creating AI systems in an ethical manner with an emphasis on responsibility, transparency, and inclusion.
- **As an illustration:**
    - *Google AI Principles:* The business is committed to developing AI systems that benefit society, refrain from fostering or enforcing unfair bias, and are accountable to individuals.
    - The complete *AI Ethical Guidelines Published by IBM* place a strong emphasis on responsibility, explainability, transparency, and justice in the development of AI.

In summary, integrating privacy, fairness, transparency, accountability, and user-centric principles across the technology lifecycle is essential to promoting ethical technology design and use. Through the implementation of tactics like Privacy by Design, explainable AI, bias detection, and ethical AI frameworks, the IT sector may produce new technologies that are also socially and fairly responsible. These initiatives guarantee that technological developments benefit society while reducing possible risks and fostering public confidence in digital networks.

Chapter 15: Future Trends in Sociology of Information Technology

15.1. Emerging Technologies and Their Societal Implications

Healthcare, banking, education, and transportation are just a few of the industries that could undergo a transformation thanks to emerging technologies like biotechnology, blockchain, artificial intelligence (AI), and quantum computing. But there are also important societal ramifications to these developments, such as moral, legal, and social issues. The detailed description of these technologies and their societal ramifications that follows is backed up by striking instances.

15.1.1. Artificial Intelligence (AI):

- **Description:** Artificial Intelligence (AI) is the programming of machines to mimic human thought processes and learning. Machine learning, computer vision, and natural language processing are examples of AI technology.
- **Social Consequences:**
    - *Job Displacement:* AI and automation may result in job displacement in industries like manufacturing and customer service where machines are more adept at performing repetitive activities.
    - *Bias and Discrimination: If* AI systems are not properly developed and supervised, they may reinforce pre-existing biases or even make them worse.
    - *Privacy Concerns:* People's right to privacy may be violated by the employment of AI in data analysis and monitoring.
- **As an illustration:**
    - *Job displacement:* To boost productivity and lessen the need for human labour in some jobs, companies

such as Amazon utilize robots driven by artificial intelligence in their warehouses.

- *Prejudice in AI:* Hiring AI systems, like those created by HireVue, have come under fire for perhaps bringing prejudice into the hiring process by giving preference to some groups of people over others.
- *Surveillance:* According to incidents documented by groups like the ACLU, AI-powered face recognition technology employed by law enforcement agencies can result in invasions of privacy and unjustified arrests.

15.1.2. Blockchain:

- **Description:** Blockchain is a decentralized ledger technology that uses distributed consensus methods and cryptographic techniques to guarantee data confidentiality and integrity.
- **Social Consequences:**
  - *Financial Inclusion:* Unbanked people can receive financial services via blockchain, especially in developing nations.
  - *Transparency and Trust:* Supply chain management and voting systems are only two areas where blockchain might improve transparency and trust.
  - *Regulatory Difficulties:* Because blockchain technology is decentralized, it might be difficult for regulatory bodies to enforce rules and regulations.
- **As an illustration:**
  - *Financial Inclusion:* Businesses such as BitPesa, which offer financial services to underprivileged areas, employ blockchain technology to make cross-border payments easier in Africa.
  - *Supply Chain Transparency:* To provide increased

supply chain transparency and traceability, Walmart tracks the provenance of food goods using blockchain technology.

- ○ *Regulation of Cryptocurrencies:* As a result of the popularity of cryptocurrencies like Bitcoin, governments are finding it difficult to create laws that forbid unlawful acts like tax evasion and money laundering.

15.1.3. The Use of Quantum Information:

- **Description:** Utilizing the ideas of quantum physics, quantum computing is able to calculate at a rate that is significantly faster than that of conventional computers.
- **Social Consequences:**
    - ○ *Cryptography*: The use of quantum computing could jeopardize internet data security by posing a threat to existing cryptography techniques.
    - ○ *Scientific Progress:* The application of quantum computing can quicken scientific progress in areas like materials science, climate modelling, and medicine development.
    - ○ *Economic Divide:* Countries and organizations that can afford the technology and those that cannot may see their economic divide widen due to the high cost and technical complexity of quantum computing.
- **As an illustration:**
    - ○ *Cryptographic Risks:* The demand for quantum-resistant cryptographic methods arose from the possibility that widely-used encryption algorithms like RSA and ECC could be broken by quantum computers.
    - ○ *Drug discovery:* Businesses like Google and IBM are

investigating how to more correctly model molecular interactions using quantum computing, which has the potential to completely transform the process of finding and developing new drugs.

15.1.4. The Internet of Things (IoT):

- **Description:** The Internet of Things (IoT) is a network of networked devices that use the internet to trade and gather data. Wearable technology, industrial sensors, and smart home appliances are some of these gadgets.
- **Social Consequences:**
    - *Security and privacy*: As IoT devices proliferate, there is a greater chance of cyberattacks and privacy violations.
    - *Data Overload*: The enormous volume of data produced by Internet of Things devices can be debilitating, necessitating sophisticated data management and analysis methods.
    - *Automation and Efficiency:* IoT can improve automation and efficiency across a range of industries, including manufacturing, healthcare, and agriculture.
- **As an illustration:**
    - *Privacy Concerns:* Due to its constant collection and transmission of user activity data, smart home appliances such as Google Nest and Amazon Echo have come under fire for possibly violating users' privacy.
    - *Industrial Internet of Things (IoT):* General Electric (GE) employs IoT sensors in its machinery to track performance and anticipate maintenance requirements, increasing productivity and decreasing

downtime.

○ *IoT in healthcare:* Fitbits and Apple Watches are just two examples of wearable technology that gathers health data, offering users and healthcare professionals useful insights but also posing privacy and data security risks.

15.1.5. Biotechnology:

- **Description:** Utilizing living things and biological systems to create goods and technologies for a range of uses, such as environmental, agricultural, and medical, is known as *biotechnology*.
- **Social Consequences**:
    ○ *Ethical Issues:* Changing genetic material creates ethical issues, especially when it comes to cloning and gene editing.
    ○ *Health and Medicine:* Advances in personalized medicine, illness prevention, and treatment can be brought about by biotechnology.
    ○ *Impact on the Environment:* Biotechnology can help with environmental problems by, for example, bioengineering crops to produce more and be more resilient to climate change.
- **As an illustration:**
    ○ *Gene editing:* Although CRISPR-Cas9 technology offers hope for the treatment of hereditary illnesses, it also presents ethical questions regarding unforeseen effects and human genetic manipulation.
    ○ *Personalized medicine:* Organizations such as 23andMe provide genetic testing services that reveal an individual's hereditary susceptibility to certain health disorders, allowing for tailored treatment

plans.

- *Bioengineered Crops:* Genetically modified crops resistant to pesticides and herbicides have been produced by Monsanto (now Bayer), increasing agricultural output but also igniting discussions over the safety and environmental effects of GMOs.

In summary, emerging technologies have enormous potential to improve healthcare, financial inclusion, efficiency, and transparency, among many other aspects of society. They do, however, also have important societal ramifications that need to be addressed properly. It is imperative to tackle matters such as employment displacement, discrimination, confidentiality, safety, and moral dilemmas to guarantee that these technologies are created and implemented appropriately. We can leverage the benefits of developing technologies while reducing their potential risks by encouraging collaboration among technologists, politicians, and society.

15.2. Challenges and Opportunities in the Future of Information Technology

Information technology (IT) has a complicated future full of possibilities and obstacles. IT workers must manage a variety of technological, moral, and social challenges as technological innovations pick up speed while taking use of new opportunities to spur creativity and improve quality of life. A detailed description of these difficulties and possibilities is provided below, backed up by striking instances.

15.2.1. The Challenges That Lie Ahead for IT

1. **Cybersecurity Threats.**

- **Description:** The techniques employed by cybercriminals also change as technology advances. Maintaining system and data security continues to be a major concern.
- **Problems:**
    - *Growing Sophistication of Attacks:* State-sponsored hacking, phishing, and ransomware are just a few examples of the complex risks that cyberattacks are posing today.
    - *Protection of Sensitive Data:* Robust protection techniques are required due to the growing amount of sensitive data, which includes financial and personal information.
    - *Cybersecurity Skills Gap:* To tackle the escalating threats, there is a deficiency of qualified cybersecurity experts.
- **As an illustration:**
    - *SolarWinds Hack:* 2020 saw a sophisticated

cyberattack against SolarWinds that resulted in the compromise of numerous important enterprises and U.S. government agencies. By inserting malicious code into SolarWinds software upgrades, the attackers were able to access confidential information.

- *Ransomware Attacks:* In 2021, an attack on the Colonial Pipeline caused fuel supply disruptions along the U.S. East Coast. This incident brought attention to the urgent need for strong cybersecurity safeguards in vital infrastructure.

1. Privacy and Ethical Issues:

- **Description:** As IT systems become more powerful and ubiquitous, protecting privacy and ensuring ethical use of technology are vital problems.
- **Problems:**
    - *Data privacy:* Protecting user privacy and adhering to laws like the CCPA and GDPR is becoming more and more difficult.
    - *AI Ethics:* The application of AI presents a number of ethical questions, such as responsibility, transparency, and bias.
- **As an illustration:**
    - *Facebook-Cambridge Analytica Scandal:* In 2018, it was discovered that Cambridge Analytica had improperly collected personal information from millions of Facebook users, raising concerns about data usage and privacy.
    - *Healthcare AI Bias:* Research has indicated that AI algorithms employed in the industry may be biased, resulting in differences in outcomes and treatment

for various populations.

1. Technological Unemployment:

- **Description:** Industries are changing due to automation and artificial intelligence (AI), which may result in job displacement and a need for worker reskilling.
- **Problems:**
    - *Job displacement:* Industries most at risk from automation include manufacturing, customer service, and transportation.
    - *Reskilling the Workforce:* Policies and procedures are required to retrain employees who have been replaced by technology.
- **As an illustration:**
    - *Automation in Manufacturing:* Employers such as Foxconn have employed robots to replace thousands of workers in their factories, boosting productivity at the expense of employment losses.
    - *Self-Driving Cars:* Businesses like Tesla and Waymo are developing self-driving cars, which might eliminate jobs for truck and taxi drivers in the transportation industry.

1. Infrastructure and Availability:

- **Description:** To promote the digital economy and close the digital divide, it is imperative to have a reliable, scalable, and easily accessible information technology infrastructure.
- **Problems:**
    - *Digital Divide:* The availability of technology and the internet varies significantly between developed and developing nations, as well as between urban and

rural areas.

- *Scalability:* Growing IT infrastructure to match the increasing demand for digital services is a major concern.

- **As an illustration:**
    - *Rural Broadband Access:* Due to the widespread lack of high-speed internet in rural areas around the United States, there are fewer options for telemedicine, remote work, and education.
    - *Global Internet Access:* Using satellite technology, projects like SpaceX's Starlink seek to address accessibility problems in remote and underdeveloped areas by offering global internet service.

15.2.2. Prospects for IT Development in the Future

1. Developments in Artificial Intelligence (AI):

- **Description:** AI still has the ability to revolutionize a number of industries by fostering efficiency and creativity.
- **Prospects:**
    - *Healthcare:* AI has the potential to enhance patient care, tailored treatment, and diagnostics.
    - *Business Operations:* AI-powered solutions may improve customer service, streamline supply chains, and encourage data-driven decision-making.
- **As an illustration:**
    - *AI in Healthcare:* By analysing medical data and helping with diagnosis and treatment planning, IBM Watson Health employs AI to potentially improve patient outcomes.
    - *AI in Customer Service:* Chatbots and virtual assistants, such as those created by IBM Watson and

ChatGPT, offer round-the-clock customer assistance, increasing productivity and client happiness.

1. **Decentralized Technologies and Blockchain:**

- **Description:** Beyond just cryptocurrencies, blockchain opens up possibilities for decentralized, transparent, and safe applications.
- **Prospects:**
    - *Supply Chain Management*: Supply chains can benefit from increased traceability and transparency thanks to blockchain.
    - *Financial Services:* More accessible and inclusive financial services can be obtained through decentralized finance, or DeFi.
- **As an illustration:**
    - *Walmart with Blockchain:* To improve food safety and transparency, Walmart tracks food products using blockchain technology from farm to store.
    - *DeFi Platforms:* By utilizing blockchain technology, platforms such as Uniswap and Compound provide decentralized financial services, such as trading and lending, without the need for conventional middlemen.

1. **Quantum Computing:**

- **Description:** Complex issues that traditional computers are unable to handle in the present day may be resolved by quantum computing.
- **Prospects:**
    - *Drug Discovery:* By simulating chemical interactions

with previously unheard-of fidelity, quantum computing can hasten the search for new medications.

- *Cryptography:* New cryptographic methods that are more resistant to future attacks can be created with quantum computing.

- **As an illustration**:
    - *Google's Quantum Supremacy:* In 2019, Google asserted its superiority over other classical supercomputers by showcasing its ability to solve a problem significantly faster using its quantum processor.
    - *Quantum Computing in Drug Discovery:* Companies like Google and IBM are investigating the use of quantum computing in the pharmaceutical industry to expedite the drug-discovery process.

1. **Internet of Things (IoT):**

- **Description:** By allowing smarter settings and improved data collection and analysis, IoT connects systems and devices.

- **Prospects:**
    - *Smart Cities:* By streamlining traffic, cutting energy use, and boosting public safety, IoT can make city life better.
    - *Healthcare:* Real-time patient health monitoring via IoT devices enables more proactive and individualized treatment.

- **As an illustration:**
    - *Smart City Initiatives:* IoT is being used by cities like Barcelona and Singapore to control traffic, save energy, and enhance public services.
    - *IoT in Healthcare:* Real-time health data is provided

by wearables like Fitbits and medical equipment like continuous glucose monitoring, which enhance patient outcomes and management.

In summary, significant potential and difficulties in the field of IT will influence how societies evolve and operate in the future. Managing the hazards associated with developing technologies will require addressing infrastructure shortages, ethical issues, technological unemployment, and cybersecurity threats. Concurrently, utilizing blockchain, quantum computing, AI, and IoT innovations offers previously unheard-of chances to improve urban life, commercial operations, healthcare, and more. Through innovation and a focus on inclusivity and ethical issues, the IT sector can propel growth that benefits all facets of society.

15.3. The Role of Sociology in Shaping Technological Futures

Technology futures are greatly influenced by sociology, the study of social behavior, institutions, and systems. Understanding the social ramifications, habits, and cultural dynamics that are influenced by technological innovations becomes crucial as technology progresses. With the help of striking examples, the following provides a comprehensive explanation of how sociology affects the creation, uptake, and effects of technology.

15.3.1. Recognizing Social Contexts:

- **An Overview**: Understanding the social environments in which technology is created and used is made easier by sociology. Examining the ways in which society norms, values, and institutions affect the uptake and consequences of technology is part of this.
- **As an illustration:**
    - *Smartphone Adoption:* By looking at how social behaviours and communication patterns have changed over time, sociologists can better understand the widespread use of cellphones. Smartphones are now essential for social contact, business, and leisure in many cultures.
    - *Social Media Platforms*: Sociological elements including people's demand for community building, identity expression, and social connection have an impact on the layout and appeal of social media sites like Facebook and Twitter.

15.3.2. Resolving Inequalities in Society:

- **Description:** Technological improvements may worsen social inequality, which sociology helps to recognize and remedy. It guarantees that technology fills gaps rather than creates new ones.
- **As an illustration:**
    - *Digital Divide*: Research from sociology emphasizes the disparity in access to technology and the internet that exists between various socioeconomic classes. By giving kids in underdeveloped nations access to inexpensive laptops, programs like One Laptop per Child seek to alleviate this issue.
    - *AI Bias*: Sociologists investigate how biases in artificial intelligence (AI) systems can maintain current societal injustices. For example, it has been discovered that individuals with darker skin tones tend to make more mistakes when using facial recognition systems, leading to calls for more fair AI design.

15.3.3. Forming Ethical Frameworks:

- **Description:** Sociology plays a role in the creation of moral frameworks that regulate technology use and make sure that advancements in technology are consistent with moral principles and societal norms.
- **As an illustration:**
    - *Data privacy*: To safeguard individual privacy in the digital era, data protection laws like GDPR are shaped by sociological insights into privacy concerns and cultural variances.
    - *AI Development Ethics:* Social science research on the effects of AI development is used to inform ethical standards, such as those put forth by the IEEE

Global Initiative on Ethics of Autonomous and Intelligent Systems.

15.3.4. Having an Impact on Technology Regulation and Policy:

- **Description:** Sociology provides politicians with information on how technology is affecting society, which helps them create laws that advance justice, security, and the general welfare.
- **As an illustration:**
    - *Net Neutrality*: The argument over net neutrality was motivated by sociological studies that highlighted the value of equitable access to online resources. As a result, laws prohibiting internet service providers from favouring particular categories of internet traffic were passed.
    - *Tech Industry Regulation:* A growing number of people are calling for regulatory actions to maintain competitive marketplaces and safeguard consumer rights as a result of sociological studies on the monopolistic behaviours of large tech businesses.

15.3.5. Encouraging Diverse Innovation:

- **Description:** Sociology fosters inclusive innovation that takes into account the demands of numerous social groups, particularly marginalized communities, by comprehending a range of social needs and behaviours.
- **As an illustration:**
    - *Assistive technology*: Sociological study on the requirements of individuals with disabilities directs the creation of assistive technology, such as screen

readers for the blind and hearing aids.

- ○ *Inclusive Design*: Tech giants such as Microsoft place a strong emphasis on inclusive design principles, making their products usable by individuals with a diverse range of talents and backgrounds.

15.3.6. Estimating the Social Effects of New Technologies:

- **Description:** In order to anticipate and lessen any potential negative effects, sociology offers methods for assessing and forecasting the social effects of new technology.
- **As an illustration:**
  - ○ *Autonomous Vehicles:* Sociologists research how autonomous vehicles may affect public transportation, urban planning, driver employment, and other societal issues. This aids in directing policy to successfully handle these changes.
  - ○ *Genetic Editing:* Sociologists examine the social ramifications of genetic editing technologies, such CRISPR, to comprehend public acceptability, potential societal stratification, and ethical problems.

15.3.7. Encouraging Public Participation and Acknowledgment:

- **Description:** Through addressing societal issues and comprehending public views, sociology helps to engage the public and promote adoption of new technology.
- **As an illustration:**
  - ○ *Public Health technology:* Sociological insights on trust, privacy issues, and social behavior have an impact on the uptake of public health technology,

such as contact tracing apps during the COVID-19 pandemic.

- *Adoption of Renewable Energy*: Designing community engagement techniques that encourage acceptance and participation is made easier by sociological studies on community views toward renewable energy projects, such solar panels and wind farms.

In summary, because sociology offers important insights into social behaviors, inequality, ethical issues, and public perceptions, it plays a crucial role in influencing the direction of technology. Technology can be designed and used in ways that are inclusive, socially responsible, and consistent with societal norms by incorporating sociological ideas. Through addressing societal demands and difficulties and promoting innovation and progress, this interdisciplinary approach guarantees that technical advancements have a positive impact on society.

15.4. The Degree to Which Women Have Adopted Information Technology to Enhance Their Standard of Living

Information technology (IT) has been adopted by women all over the world to enhance their standard of living and make a substantial contribution to social, economic, and personal advancement. This adoption is being implemented in a number of sectors, including as community development, business, education, and health. The detailed explanation and striking instances of how women are using IT to improve their lives are provided below.

15.4.1. Education and Developing Skills:

- **Platforms for Online Learning:**
    - Women have used online learning environments such as edX, Khan Academy, and Coursera to further their professions and acquire new skills.
    - **Example:** Google's "Women in Tech" program in India helps women enter the IT industry by offering them online training in digital skills.
- **Bootcamps for Coders:**
    - Coding bootcamps and courses are provided by organizations like Girls Who Code and Women Who Code to encourage women to work in the tech industry.
    - **Example:** The American Ada Developers Academy helps women—especially those from marginalized backgrounds—secure employment in the technology sector by offering them extensive training and internships.

15.4.2. Economic Empowerment and Entrepreneurship:

- **Internet and e-commerce businesses:**
  - Overcoming conventional hurdles to market access, women have embraced e-commerce platforms such as Etsy, eBay, and Shopify to launch and expand their home-based companies.
  - **Example:** the "She Leads Africa" initiative in Nigeria offers training in internet marketing, sales, and business management to assist female entrepreneurs in using digital resources to grow their companies.
- **Digital Financial Services:**
  - Women are now more capable of managing their money, saving, and investing thanks to the availability of digital financial services via mobile banking and fintech solutions.
  - **Example:** M-Pesa has completely changed financial inclusion in Kenya, where a large number of women use mobile money services to save for the future of their families and operate small enterprises.

15.4.3. Health and Well-Being:

- **Telemedicine:**
  - Telemedicine services facilitate quick medical consultations and lessen travel requirements for women residing in distant and disadvantaged locations by offering healthcare access.
  - **Example:** To ensure that pregnant women in remote places receive prenatal care and guidance from medical specialists, the "Maternova" platform provides telehealth services.
- **Health Education and Information:**

- ○ Women may make educated decisions about their health and wellbeing by using the essential health information provided by internet resources and mobile apps.
  - ○ **Example:** The Maternity Foundation's "Safe Delivery App" helps improve maternal health outcomes by providing expectant women and midwives in poor nations with guidelines and educational videos.

15.4.4. Social and Community:

- **Social Media for Advocacy:**
  - ○ Women campaign for social causes, spread awareness, and organize communities via social media sites like Facebook, Instagram, and Twitter.
  - ○ **Example:** The #MeToo movement, which grew in popularity on social media, has given women the confidence to speak out against sexual harassment and assault, which has resulted in important global social and legal changes.
- **Internet-Based Support Communities:**
  - ○ Online forums and communities offer resources and assistance to women dealing with a range of issues, from career advancement to parenthood.
  - ○ **Example:** websites such as "Mumsnet" and "The Mom Project" provide job possibilities and discussion boards for mothers, assisting them in the juggling of work and family obligations.

15.4.5. Networking with Professionals to Advance Your Career

- **Professional Groups and LinkedIn:**
    - ○ Women can increase their career chances by connecting with mentors, peers, and possible employers through LinkedIn and other professional networking platforms.
    - ○ **Example:** "Ellevate Network" is a global professional women's network that works to advance women in the workplace by offering events, resources, and mentorship opportunities through online platforms.
- **Possibilities for Remote Work:**
    - ○ Women now have more job options because to the growth of remote work, especially those who require flexible schedules since they are responsible for caring for others.
    - ○ **Example:** organizations such as "Remote.co" and "FlexJobs" provide a list of remote job openings, enabling women to locate work that works with their schedules.

In summary, information technology has been adopted by women to greatly improve their lives in a variety of fields. Women are breaking through conventional boundaries and establishing new opportunities for themselves and their communities by using professional networks, telemedicine, digital company startups, social advocacy, and online education. In addition to giving women more economic power, the transformative potential of IT has also raised their social status, health, and educational attainment, all of which have benefited from greater societal advancement. The potential for more good effects on women's lives is enormous as technology develops, offering a more inclusive and equal future.

Conclusion

In summary, although often unsettling, the shifts influencing the interaction between science, engineering, and society are setting the stage for that connection in the twenty-first century. The future of science, technology, and society cannot be fully predicted. However, by extracting from significant current trends, we can expect science, engineering, and society to become even more interdependent.

Some of the difficulties that would arise from this interconnectedness are also imaginable. Thanks to technological advancements, industrial productivity will keep rising and benefit economies, consumers, and enterprises in various ways. However, increased productivity may result in fewer jobs rather than more.

For instance, because to the high productivity of American agriculture, the country has transitioned from being primarily occupied by farmers to one where 3.6% of all Americans are able to grow enough food to feed everyone in the nation as well as export it. Technological advancements are known to be a powerful source of new jobs, but they can also cause temporary job displacement. Where will the future workforce be employed and what skill-sets will they need to possess?

The ways in which we work, learn, and communicate with one another will all be altered by information technologies. It's possible that several of these technologies will make it to the most isolated locations on the planet. To what ends will these technologies be used, and by whom will they be controlled? These are begging questions.

Industries focused on science and technology will keep expanding globally. Governments will compete with one another in all areas of research and development in an effort to promote the creation of new knowledge and proprietary goods. For instance, the Asia and Pacific nations, which historically primarily relied on technology transfer from other nations, are steadily increasing their fundamental research capacities even as they maintain their emphasis on technical advancement. How will nations who are unable to establish cutting-edge industries or research capacities compete? What mechanism will be put in place to ensure inclusivity?

As information technology become more and more integrated into instruction, all levels of education will experience radical transformations. Children who are unable to benefit from new technology run the risk of falling behind, globally. What consequences might a move away from conventional education have in the long run? What mitigating factors must be put in place to ensure all children from all digital-divide receive a decent education?

These are challenging questions for which there are currently no satisfactory answers. However, they make it very evident that as science-driven technologies gain prominence, they will revolutionize how people interact, transact business, and live their lives. Both the rate of technical advancement and the uptake of new technologies, as well as the rate of scientific discovery, are increasing. These new technologies will alter human existence in some disruptive ways, but they also have the potential to significantly raise our standard of living.

FAQS

1. **What is Sociology of Information Technology?**

- **Answer:** *The social dimensions of IT creation, use, and implementation are examined by sociology of information technology. It investigates the relationship between society and technology. Social media sites like Facebook and Twitter, for instance, have revolutionized communication and had an impact on everything from political movements to interpersonal relationships.*

1. **How does social interactions be impacted by Information Technology?**

- **Answer:** *Information technology has an impact on social relationships by giving people new means of collaboration, communication, and connection. For example, real-time communication across the globe is made possible by messaging apps like WhatsApp, which may both disrupt and reinforce traditional face-to-face interactions while also fostering connections despite physical distance.*

1. **How does IT influence the design of contemporary workplaces?**

- **Answer:** *IT is essential to current work environments because it makes remote work possible, automates activities, and boosts output. Virtual meetings and collaboration are made possible by apps like Zoom and Slack, which let teams work effectively from anywhere. However, they also bring up issues with work-life balance and continuous connectivity.*

1. **How does IT affect the disparities in society?**

- **Answer:** *IT has the ability to both reduce and increase social inequality. While not having access to technology can worsen already-existing inequality, it can also present opportunities for education and the economy. For instance, students who had access to dependable internet and gadgets during the COVID-19 outbreak were able to complete their coursework online, while others who did not had these facilities fell behind.*

1. **Describe the Digital Divide and explain its importance.**

- **Answer:** *The difference between people who have access to contemporary information and communication technologies and those who do not is known as the "digital divide." This gap matters because it has an impact on opportunities for employment, education, and information access. For example, inhabitants in rural areas are sometimes unable to fully participate in the digital economy due to a lack of high-speed internet.*

1. **How do IT policies impact Surveillance and Privacy?**

- **Answer:** *The answer is that IT facilitates mass data collecting and monitoring, which has an impact on privacy and surveillance. Social networking sites, for instance, gather a tonne of personal information about users in order to target ads, and businesses and governments utilize surveillance technologies to track user activity, which raises moral and legal questions regarding users' right to privacy.*

1. **How does IT affect the educational process?**

- **Answer:** *IT changes education by making new learning*

resources and tools available, enabling online learning, and facilitating distant learning. Access to educational content is made possible by platforms such as Coursera and Khan Academy, which democratize education while also emphasizing the importance of digital literacy and infrastructure.

1. **In what ways does IT support globalization?**

- **Answer:** *The quick interchange of resources and information made possible by IT connections between individuals and enterprises across borders is one way that it promotes globalization. Businesses can access foreign markets through e-commerce sites like Amazon, and cloud services facilitate cross-border cooperation that promotes trade and cultural exchanges.*

1. **How does Artificial Intelligence (AI) affect society in terms of Ethics?**

- **Answer:** *Worries over employment displacement, privacy, decision-making biases, and responsibility are among the ethical implications of AI. Artificial intelligence (AI) algorithms employed in the employment process, for instance, may inadvertently reinforce prejudices found in the training set, resulting in discriminatory recruiting practices.*

1. **How does IT affect people's engagement in politics?**

- **Answer:** *IT affects political engagement by offering fresh venues for advocacy, activism, and information sharing. In movements such as the Arab Spring, social media has been essential in helping organizers gather support and disseminate information quickly. However, it has also presented obstacles in the form of false information and echo chambers.*

1. **How does IT fit into the healthcare industry?**

- **Answer:** *Information technology (IT) improves patient records management, makes telemedicine easier, and makes advanced data analysis possible for more accurate diagnosis and treatment. While telehealth services increase access to care, particularly in underprivileged areas, electronic health records (EHRs) enhance the effectiveness and accuracy of patient information.*

1. **How does IT impact the Evolution of Culture?**

- **Answer:** *The rapid dissemination of ideas and cultural practices across borders is how IT influences cultural transformation. Netflix and other streaming services provide a worldwide audience with access to a wide range of content, which shapes cultural norms and perceptions while also posing concerns about cultural uniformity and the erasure of regional customs.*

1. **How does an Addiction to social media affect society?**

- **Answer:** *An addiction to social media can result in detrimental effects on mental health, including despair, anxiety, and low self-esteem. It may also have an impact on productivity and relationships in real life. For instance, overuse of social media sites like Instagram can exacerbate problems with body image and social comparison.*

1. **What is the effect of IT breakthroughs on employment?**

- **Answer:** *The development of IT has the potential to both create and destroy jobs. While AI and automation might create new opportunities in tech and other growing professions, they can also replace regular work and result in job displacement in some* *sectors. For example, the growth of IT has reduced the necessity for some manual labour occupations while increasing the demand for cybersecurity professionals.*

1. **How does IT affect the way that consumers behave?**

- **Answer:** *IT affects customer behavior by enabling online transactions and offering customized purchasing experiences. E-commerce websites make buying more convenient by using algorithms to suggest products based on browsing history and likes, but this also raises privacy issues about data usage.*

1. **How does IT affect interpersonal relationships?**

- **Answer:** *IT affects interpersonal relationships in two ways: it makes communication and connection possible all the time, but it also poses problems like digital reliance and a decline in in-person contacts. Social media sites like Facebook facilitate communication, but because they don't provide nonverbal clues, they can also cause miscommunication and conflict.*

1. **How will IT influence cities in the future?**

- **Answer:** *The creation of smart cities, which leverage technology to enhance public services, transportation, and infrastructure, is how IT impacts the future of cities. Smart traffic management systems that lessen traffic jams and Internet of Things (IoT) devices that improve resource management and public safety are two examples.*

1. **How does information technology affect international security?**

- **Answer:** *IT has a big impact on international security because of things like data breaches, cyberattacks, and the use of technology in combat. Attacks against infrastructure, as the 2021 Colonial Pipeline hack, highlight cybersecurity's weaknesses and its effects on national security, making it a major worry.*

1. **How may IT impact the dynamics of a family?**

- **Answer:** *The way that IT modifies family members' interactions and communication has an impact on family dynamics. Long-distance family connections are made possible by technologies like video calls, but excessive smartphone and device use can also result in less face-to-face engagement and quality time spent together as a family.*

1. **How does IT fit into the fight against climate change?**

- **Answer:** *Information technology (IT) facilitates improved resource management, data analysis, and monitoring. For instance, smart grids and energy management systems maximize resource utilization and lower carbon footprints, while environmental sensors and data analytics support climate patterns and guide sustainable behaviors.*

Table of Figures

Bibliography

1. Mattern, Friedemann; Floerkemeier, Christian (2010). "From the Internet of Computers to the Internet of Things". From Active Data Management to Event-Based Systems and More. Lecture Notes in Computer Science. Vol. 6462. pp. 242–259. ISBN 978-3-642-17225-0.

2. Weber, Rolf H. (2010). "Internet of Things – New security and privacy challenges". Computer Law & Security Review. 26 (1): 23–30. ISSN 0267-3649. S2CID 6968691.

3. Joan Ferrante-Wallace, Joan Ferrante, Sociology.net: Sociology on the Internet, Thomson Wadsworth, 1996, ISBN 9780534527563

4. Carla G. Surratt, "The Internet and Social Change", McFarland, 2001, ISBN 978-0786410194

5. Baber, Zaheer (1992). Ashmore, Malcolm; Bhaskar, Roy; Mukerji, Chandra; Woolgar, Steve; Yearley, Steven (eds.). "Sociology of Scientific Knowledge: Lost in the Reflexive Funhouse?". Theory and Society. 21 (1): 105–119. ISSN 0304-2421.

6. Mukosha Patrick (2023), "Unleashing the Power of Inclusive Innovation: Transforming the World for All"; GoodMan Series, ISBN 9798223009269

Don't miss out!

Visit the website below and you can sign up to receive emails whenever Patrick Mukosha publishes a new book. There's no charge and no obligation.

https://books2read.com/r/B-A-HJNZ-VOKID

Did you love *"The Sociology of Information Technology"*? Then you should read *"Careers in Information Technology: Cybersecurity Analyst"*[1] by Patrick Mukosha!

In **"Careers in Information Technology: *Cybersecurity Analyst,*"** readers are introduced to the vital and ever-changing topic of cybersecurity in a perceptive manner. This thorough guide delves into the fascinating field of cybersecurity, illuminating the many prospects, difficulties, and routes to success in this highly sought-after profession.

Because businesses, governments, and individuals rely on the security of their digital assets and data, cybersecurity has emerged as a fundamental component of the contemporary digital era. This book offers a thorough examination of the job of a cybersecurity analyst while diving into the complexities of the cybersecurity industry.

---

1. https://books2read.com/u/496DOJ

2. https://books2read.com/u/496DOJ

The basic question of what a cybersecurity analyst is and does is addressed at the outset of the book. Readers will acquire a comprehensive comprehension of the duties, abilities, and expertise necessary to succeed in this position. Cybersecurity analysts are essential to protecting sensitive data, from spotting security problems to putting preventative measures in place.

The educational and career paths that lead to becoming a cybersecurity analyst will also be examined by readers. The book provides advice on training courses, degrees, and certifications that prospective professionals can take to get started in this sector. It also emphasizes how crucial it is to keep up with the always changing cybersecurity scene and how ongoing learning is essential to maintaining effectiveness in the position.

The theoretical parts of the book are not the only ones covered. It offers helpful insights into the day-to-day activities of a cybersecurity analyst. The technology and techniques utilized by cybersecurity experts, such as firewalls, intrusion detection systems, and threat intelligence platforms, will be transparently shown to readers.

For anybody interested in a career in cybersecurity or wanting to learn more about the vital role cybersecurity analysts play in safeguarding our digital world, **"Careers in Information Technology: *Cybersecurity Analyst,*"** is a must-read. This book is an invaluable tool for anyone starting this exciting career journey because it provides practical knowledge, a road map for success, and an outlook on the future.

Whether you're an IT enthusiast, a student, or a career changer, this book offers the support and motivation you need to succeed in the fast-paced world of cybersecurity.

Also by Patrick Mukosha

GoodMan
Resilient Strategies: Thriving in Harsh Business Conditions
Strategic Entrepreneurship: Navigating The Path To Success
Decisive Power: Navigating How to Make Toughest Decisions
"Reigning the Boardroom: A Trailblazing Guide to Corporate Governance Success"
Fortifying Digital Fortress: A Comprehensive Guide to Information Systems Security
"Unleashing the Power of Inclusive Innovation: Transforming the World for All"
"Exploring Computer Systems: From Fundamentals to Advanced Concepts"
"Computer Viruses Unveiled: Types, Trends and Mitigation Strategies"
"The Pinnacle of Success: Unveiling the World's 20 Most Successful Brands in 2023"
"Mastering Relational Databases: From Fundamentals to Advanced Concepts"
"Navigating Change: A Comprehensive Guide to Change Management"
"Information Systems Unraveled: Exploring the Core Concepts"
"Careers in Information Technology: Network Engineer"

"Careers in Information Technology: Network and Systems Administrator"
"Careers in Information Technology: Database Administrator"
"Careers in Information Technology: Cybersecurity Analyst"
"Careers in Information Technology: Cloud Security Specialist"
"Careers in Information Technology: Blockchain Developer"
"Careers in Information Technology: DevOps Engineer"
"Careers in Information Technology: Quality Assurance Analyst"
"Careers in Information Technology: Machine Learning Engineer"
"Careers in Information Technology: Artificial Intelligence (AI) Engineer"
"Careers in Information Technology: Internet of Things (IoT) Developer"
"Careers in Information Technology: AR/VR Developer"
"Careers in Information Technology: IoT Embedded Systems Designer"
"Careers in Information Technology: Artificial Intelligence (AI) Robotics Engineer"
"Careers in Information Technology: IoT Solutions Engineer"
"Careers in Information Technology: Data Scientist"
"Careers in Information Technology: Computer Vision Engineer"
"The Sociology of Information Technology"